The DARTNELL/ANDERSON 20-POINT SYSTEM for <u>GUARANTEED</u> SALES SUCCESS

by George B. Anderson

 DARTNELL

To my son, Stuart, a salesman
on whom I'm thoroughly sold.

Contents

4

Get System Into Your Selling

Good amateurs may win laurels, but it's the pro who gets the money. And it's not only more profitable but it's more fun to do anything well than to do it poorly.

Then why are there so many really bad salesmen? Why be inept when it's so much more satisfactory to be an expert?

Most poor salesmen are inefficient because nobody's ever taught them the simple basics of selling. They've been given product information or service information until it's running out of their ears. They know spec sheets and data. But nobody's taught them how to open a sales solicitation, how to make it progress smoothly, how to answer objections, and, vitally important, how to close a sale.

Far too much has been written about the "gift" of salesmanship—and this book won't add to the accumulation. The more I see of salesmen, the more convinced I am that those who depend on the gift or knack of selling really depend on luck. The good salesman knows what he's doing and why he's doing it. He's a pro.

I can't deny that there's sometimes a psychic element in selling, but the value of the "hunch" has been vastly overrated. Granted that a top salesman knows instinctively when to do certain things to close a sale, you still must admit that there's nothing mysterious about his ability to dominate a solicitation and create a situation where his hunches will work.

And if the Instinct Boys leave me cold, I'm equally unimpressed by the Busy Bees, the salesmen who run up maximum mileage and make tremendous numbers of calls.

"Give me a man who makes enough calls," my first boss, a newspaper advertising manager, told me, "and I know he'll make sales. I'd rather have a beginner who makes 50 calls a day than an experienced salesman who makes five."

At the time that sales philosophy was directed my way, I didn't know it was rubbish. It's been said so often that repetition has created belief in some quarters. I almost believed it, myself, until I saw the theory put to practice.

I've since seen salesmen who could ruin all chances for future sales with one, quick, brisk, bumbling call—who could make solicitations from now 'til next year without creating any business—and who could sometimes actually prompt cancellation of orders that were already in the mail.

Hustle and energy are great qualities, no question about it, but they're not enough to make a good salesman any more than they make a good doctor or a good lawyer. A first-rate salesman knows the rules of selling and how to apply them to every prospect.

At least, he knows *some* of the rules and applies *some* of them.

People have been selling ever since Eve did a sales job on Adam. From the billions of dollars' worth of sales consummated in modern times, there should be evidence on the relative merits of various sales techniques—and there is. Unfortunately, few people take the time to examine that evidence or, having studied it, to apply it to their own selling problems.

Mail order advertisers have checked the efficiency of their selling copy for many years. From copy-testing experiments, they know that one approach may be several hundred percent better than another. They know that failure to include certain selling elements can wreck results, so they maintain "check" systems to insure against forgetfulness or carelessness.

Many great retail advertisers have installed their own secret advertising check systems—and most good advertising agencies, whether they admit it or not, grade their advertising copy against a checklist of tested, proven advertising appeals.

7

Now, obviously, no checklist can transform an incompetent copy-writer into a wizard with words. It can't put sparkling, sales-compelling ideas into his mind. All it can do—and what it *does* do—is promote orderly thinking and serve as a watchdog to see that every necessary element of good sales copy is included in each advertisement.

To show an extreme example, a mail-order ad that carries the name and address of the advertiser is certainly going to get more results than one that doesn't. And yet, some advertisements forget elements that are almost as important as the place to send the money.

Oral Need Is Greater

If sales copy needs a checklist, *oral* salesmanship needs it even more. It is far easier for a salesman, talking and demonstrating his way toward a sale, to forget or overlook some basic part of a good sales presentation than it is for the copywriter, working under less pressure. The salesman must operate in a greater latitude, and his approach must be conditioned by the reactions of his prospective customer. In trying to answer certain objections and prove specific things about his product or service, it's the easiest thing in the world for him to overlook vital parts of a good selling job.

My experience with check systems began on The Chicago *Tribune* at the time Will Townsend was creating a furor in the advertising field with his "Townsend 27 Points." Advertising agencies whose personnel wasn't already using a check system didn't like the idea at all, and said so.

The *Tribune* was interested. I was assigned to work with Clyde Bedell on a check system for retail advertising copy, and later, when the *Tribune* bought the rights to the Townsend check system, it was my job to condense, simplify and revise it into a 90-minute oral presentation.

Chicago advertisers were wary of the check system—until they saw it. Then they found that the aura of mystery surrounding it was simply a glamorous selling tool. The ideas in the check system, they agreed, made excellent sense.

After considerable work with the late Art Martin and his Sales Training Institute, it was inevitable that I should get the idea of applying the check system to personal selling.

I went to experts for help. Four of the six men who helped me have expressly forbidden the use of their names—and I understand how they feel about it. Getting a reputation as an above-average salesman can be a dangerous thing. I've never forgotten Hugh Carter.

Hugh was whipping the sox off his competitors, all through his territory. The other salesmen became so desperate that they held a council of war which resulted in this kind of strategy.

John Downey, one of Hugh's competitors, would make a call. "There's just one question," he would say in opening. "Has Hugh Carter called on you? If he has, I know I'm just wasting my time trying to sell you. If you haven't already bought, you've at least decided you're going to give him an order. The guy is just too good. At least, I'm not a good enough salesman to compete with him. Ordinarily, I have plenty of confidence in my own ability—but not when Hugh's around. He can sell anybody anything."

Every competing salesman used the same technique, and in six months, Hugh Carter's potential customers were afraid to say hello to him. Within a year, he went into a different territory with a new line.

The Men Behind the System

The men who've helped me don't deserve to be put into that kind of a jam, but I do want you to know about them and why I've taken so much of their advice.

One of them, "The Roughneck," never went past the sixth grade in public school. He started selling from door to door as a youngster and kept right on selling to the point where he became a top sales management executive. The Roughneck is a man who has tested every sales approach in the field and who accepts only one sales solicitation—the one that gets the order. He is tough and enthusiastic, the kind of person who refuses to accept disappointment or failure. He's considered a difficult employer.

"The Competitor" is a sales manager who actually dislikes soft jobs. He stays in one post only until he's licked the problems, and then jumps to another position. It's invariably a job with tougher problems—and greater financial rewards. He's a ruthless driver, but pays handsomely for the men who fulfill his exacting requirements. He's a keen analyst of product weaknesses and how to overcome them.

Trial and Error Experiments

"The Scientist" is a sales manager who regards the business world as his laboratory. He conducts many sales experiments, keeps accurate records of sales approaches and gives his men the full benefit of his findings. This fellow makes "trial and error" sales solicitations pay off so well that when he says a certain plan will bring in a certain number of dollars, his sales force wouldn't bet a dime against his estimate.

"The Boy Wonder" became sales manager of an important firm while he was in his early thirties. A graduate of an excellent school of business administration, he is a firm believer in applied psychology in salesmanship. The Boy Wonder is positive that knowing and understanding your customers is just as important as knowledge of your product. His men swear by him, and some of them who are older than he give him their unqualified respect and loyalty.

"The Personality Kid" is a sales manager who knows every customer by first name or nickname and has developed genuine friendships with all of them. He gets more visible fun from his work than most men. Outsiders sometimes make the mistake of classifying him as shallow—but he's a key man in advertising conferences, product design consultation, policy meetings and almost every other phase of his company's business. The president of the company realizes that The Personality Kid knows what his customers want. His sales force has a number of "exclusive" customers that is far above normal.

"The Old Timer" is a sales manager who's remained active past retirement age because his men insisted that they needed him. He has been through enough booms and busts so that nothing really panics him, and nobody can suggest a method of stimulating sales that he hasn't used at one time or another. His men love him, although he's a hard taskmaster. He violently dislikes the young man who refuses to regard selling as a profession and a life career.

These are the six men who helped me in the formation of the Dartnell/Anderson 20-Point System for Guaranteed Sales Success. They know what they're talking about and have bank balances to prove it.

Four of them went into the creation of the system without any real enthusiasm—and soon sold themselves on it. All six now agree that any salesman who will use the 20 Points and check his solicitations against them will improve his work and his results.

When I began doing work with the Sales Training Institute, I was dumbfounded by some of the people who were solidly successful as sales trainers. They had never sold anything in their lives except sales training material—and some of what they sold should have been against the law.

Began Sales Career at 13

Back when I was 13 years old, I was doing house-to-house selling—and I don't mean seeds or greeting cards. When I was 15, I was successfully selling knit ties by mail.

Driving automobiles "blindfolded" (a magician's ancient trick), paid my way through college. The "blindfold drive" was a newspaper exploitation stunt, with about 20 advertisers involved in the average drive. The results were magnificent. As the money rolled in, it finally occurred to me that I was making this money not by driving automobiles blindfolded but by selling newspapers and merchants on the returns they would get from participation in the stunt.

11

This was one-shot, hit-and-run selling of a type that's seldom seen today. You couldn't fool yourself with the thought that you'd make a sale on a call-back. There wasn't going to be any call-back. There wasn't time for one. You had to walk in cold and make a sale—if you wanted that beautiful money.

When I was 17 years old, getting ready for my sophomore year in college, I was making more money during the 12 or 13 weeks of summer vacation than some solid citizens were getting for a year's work. It was tremendous experience, because there was no tomorrow. And since there was no second chance, I had to be daring in my sales approach. If I felt I was flubbing a sale, there wasn't any reason to avoid a wild, unorthodox approach. And I found that some of those approaches worked, so I used them again.

Too Much Money Coming

My first job after college was selling so-called "special" advertising on the Sioux City (Iowa) *Tribune*—on a commission basis. Gene Kelly, the business manager, gave me a generous commission arrangement and after I'd worked for three weeks, I asked him if I could get a little of the money I had coming.

"Of course," he said. "You can get it all." He took me to the cashier's office and asked, "Art, Does George have any money coming?"

"He sure does," Art replied.

"How much?"

"A little over three thousand dollars," the cashier replied.

"Good Lord," Gene said. "Kid, you've got to go to work on a salary right now." In a couple of months, not yet 21 years old, I was classified manager of this paper with 60,000 circulation. The opposition paper had the lead in classified, so the selling was rough and tough.

Then I ran a country weekly newspaper and did a sales promotion job that I wouldn't want to try again. I sold over 50 special advertising promotions in one year.

From there, I went to the Aurora (Ill.) *Beacon-News* as an advertising salesman, and had the privilege of working under a great salesman, Charles Hoefer. I was long gone by the time Charlie was made publisher of the paper, but I'm still proud of his offering me his old job as advertising director. I couldn't afford to take it, because meanwhile I'd moved ahead rather rapidly.

I had become manager of The Chicago *Tribune* Newspaper Advertising Service, a syndicated copy-and-art service for newspapers, with a sales force covering the United States.

While on that job, I accidentally got into the radio field. W. Biggie Levin, a fine talent agent, soon convinced me that I could no longer afford the luxury of my full-time job at the *Tribune,* and I began devoting my whole time to the creation and sale of radio shows, followed by television shows.

Through that work, I got into the advertising agency business, where I've now spent a good many years. I started the first sales-training department in any advertising agency in this country, because I felt it was a vitally important area of service.

Wherever I've been, I've always had to sell. I've made a good many big sales, including a few million-dollar ones, and quite a few hundred-thousand-dollar sales. Some of the most difficult have been much smaller sales. Maybe one reason is that you—at least I—plan much more carefully for the big ones than for the small ones.

A Shortage of Good Salesmen

I've always taken selling seriously. I've always studied it. If I were going to sell, I preferred being a pro to being an amateur. And I decided early in the game that selling could be learned—that using your head could pay handsome dividends.

Today, there's great concern on the part of many top manufacturers over a serious shortage of candidates for important sales managerial positions. Executives in many companies don't feel that their current salesmen have the capability to fill the jobs that are opening. The problem is made worse by a falling off in the male population in the 35-to-44 age bracket.

Present field salesmen should be ideal candidates for jobs as executives. Since many companies don't feel that their field men are potential sales managers, something must be wrong with those companies' sales organizations.

Some Men Resist Change

Perhaps the men have resisted advancement and the change which progress always involves. I've had men working for me who fought change with everything they had. You sometimes have to force men into progress—but it can be done, and a good sales manager can do it, even though it irks him that he needs to push his men into bettering themselves.

Most often, in my experience, the reason for a lack of potential sales managers on the current staff is simply that their training has been inadequate—sometimes pitifully inadequate.

And this isn't always the sales manager's fault, by a long shot. Top management in some companies puts such restrictions on sales management that the man who could do a good training job would have to be a miracle worker.

Boards of directors, some of their membership far removed from sales field reality, have thought sales costs were too high from the time selling began. It's hard to get through to these men the fact that sales costs are highest where the men are the most poorly trained.

Men with great potentials in selling are sometimes ruined by being thrown into the major league of selling with no bush league experience and inadequate coaching.

No man can do a good job without confidence in his ability as a salesman. Many a salesman who wouldn't admit it under penalty of torture is completely lacking in self-confidence. He knows that he doesn't know how to sell. He senses that he's never learned the basic principles of selling and feels that his sales depend on the law of averages rather than his own sales ability.

The sales manager we call The Roughneck says, "When top management is screaming about the lack of potential executives in the field, how in blazes would you expect the salesmen to have any confidence?

"All too often, there's a company attitude that a sales force is a necessary evil that has to be tolerated but shouldn't be encouraged. You gotta have salesmen, but you don't have to like it. And that attitude comes through loud and clear to the men, don't think it doesn't. The salesmen aren't even kept informed of what's going on in the company. The sales manager can't do the job because he isn't informed, either.

"A lot of this top brass that yips so loud needs to take a look at the home office to find out why the salesmen aren't doing better. One of our competitors, for example, has a good bunch of men—but we're robbing them of business because the company doesn't fill orders on schedule. The word 'Rush' on an order is almost a challenge to somebody in that outfit to see how long he can hold up shipment.

"We've got another competitor with a lousy service organization. They take their sweet time shipping parts and they do stinking work on machines that need repairs. Where does that leave their salesmen? I'll tell you where—right out in left field."

Many Need Encouragement

At one session, The Scientist took a direct pot-shot at The Roughneck.

"Sometimes," he said, "potentially good men are ruined by sales managers. There are tough sales managers who seem to think there's something soft about giving a salesman a pat on the back for a job well done—and if anybody in the world needs such encouragement, it's a salesman out on the road.

15

"Another place where some sales managers spoil good men is in unbalanced territories. One man has all the 'gravy' business and another faces a really tough selling job that needs to be preceded by much missionary work. I've found that while money and benefits will motivate salesmen, their enthusiasm is kept alive more by encouraging results, evidence that they're moving ahead."

"You baby your men," The Roughneck answered. "Everybody knows that you practically wet-nurse 'em. A good salesman needs to have a tough hide. If he's gonna cry every time he misses an order, he oughta get out of selling."

"But he doesn't get out," The Scientist said. "He does just well enough to stay on the payroll. The lackadaisical salesman's attitude gives buyers the idea that the entire company must have a what-the-hell attitude. You can't really sell without enthusiasm."

"I keep 'em enthused," The Roughneck said, "with the best enthuser there is—a prod from the rear."

"Gentlemen," I said, "we're getting afield. We are all agreed on one thing—that every company needs a good, basic sales training program that takes nothing for granted—a program that teaches the proof points, certainly—but one that goes far beyond that in teaching the things that make sales possible in any field, at any time. We *are* agreed on that, aren't we?"

Everybody said, "Right!"

What This System for Selling Can Do

The Dartnell/Anderson 20-Point System for Guaranteed Sales Success covers every element in a theoretically perfect sales presentation. No sales expert to date, after study of the points, can think of anything to add or will suggest eliminating any point. It's all there—every rule or secret or truth that goes to make a sale.

One of my associates was arranging a seminar on the system with a substantial and successful Wisconsin company. "Yes, it's all there," the sales manager said, "but so much of it is fundamental."

"That's quite right," my associate nodded. "I know you think the Green Bay Packers are quite a ball club. They're playing for the championship next Sunday. And I read in the paper at breakfast that this football team, probably the best in the world at the moment, has spent two days this week on fundamentals."

My system is no magic formula and I'd be the last to claim any genius for its creation. You're already familiar with most of the elements to be found in it.

What it does that hasn't been done before is to put everything known about a good sales solicitation into a system of selling through orderly thinking and action. It's a guide to prompt a salesman to do all the things he should do to transact the maximum amount of business. It can bring out the best selling abilities of every man who takes his selling job seriously enough to try to improve his work.

The rules apply, no matter what you're selling—a product or a service. They make sense in any selling situation.

One of the key secrets of the 20-Point System is self-evaluation. The system gives *you* as a salesman a definite, clean-cut method of evaluating your own sales solicitations and methods of handling them.

It's a rare individual who can look at himself objectively. We're too close to ourselves to do a completely fair, impartial job of self-criticism. And being able to recognize your own weaknesses is a great asset. Once you recognize your shortcomings, it's usually possible to show notable improvement.

During the development of the system, we made a survey of salesmanship on both products and services, with salesmen judged on the basis of the 20-Point System and with a possible perfect rating of 100%. This random survey showed an overall rating of 25% efficiency in selling.

Half Sell By Luck, Instinct

Four percent of the men surveyed knew their jobs well. Nearly half were selling by luck and instinct, and of these, 15% knew virtually nothing about selling. Forty percent knew something but only a small part of their jobs. Only 2% of the men could be called complete misfits—but every man could have benefited from familiarity with the 20 basic points of selling. The average could have benefited nearly 300%!

With this system for selling, a salesman can, in two or three minutes following a sales interview, know what kind of a job he did, where he excelled and where he fell down. He can, I hope, often find out instantly how to make a call-back get results where the first approach failed.

Habit in following the checklist should get you to the point where it will be virtually impossible for a prospective customer to confuse you. But let me emphasize, you improve yourself through your own efforts. The system makes you a pro by teaching you how to use the sales ability and tools you already possess. It's no cure-all for sales ineffectiveness but a guide to the best selling job you can do.

There is obviously one best basic sales solicitation for every item and every service, just as there's one best approach for a specific type of customer. By the time you're familiar with this system and have learned how to apply it, every sales solicitation you make can be the best you're capable of making.

But there's a hook. It isn't the points in themselves but the right *application* of each selling point to your specific selling problem that's important. Only when you apply the points do they go to work for you.

As the points are given to you, one at a time, your first job will be to decide how each point applies to you, to your product or service, and to your customers. Every point requires thought. You must figure out how to make each one do maximum duty for you.

Once you're satisfied that you understand the application of all 20 points, you'll be ready to use the checklist. With it, you'll check yourself and help yourself. Whenever you complete a selling solicitation, you'll check against the 20 Points. You'll ask yourself which points you covered and which ones you missed—which you handled well and which ones you handled poorly.

Try It for 30 Days

If you use the checklist every day for 30-days, you will have acquired selling habits that will stick with you for the rest of your life. If you think about the points and try to improve your application of them, you'll become a real pro.

Each point is an assistant that can help you to close sales. If you acquire only one point, you'll be a better salesman than you were before.

Only a few people are mentally, physically or temperamentally unfitted to the profession of selling. Some people don't take the problems of selling seriously enough. Some are too lazy. You might be surprised to know how many people don't like any kind of work at all. The only problem most of us have, though, is that we try to succeed without following the basic rules of success.

There's a good reason why the 20 Points of this selling system aren't included in list form in the opening pages of this book. The list would be confusing and almost meaningless if you were to get it before you understand each point and its application to you. Don't worry. You'll get a list of the points when you're ready for it. For now, let it suffice to say that the 20 Points are divided into four main sections: PERSONAL, PROOF, OPPOSITION, and CLOSE. Don't worry about those classifications, either, or even try to analyze them until you reach them.

Make Each Point Apply

Your job right now is going to be to try to make each point apply to you as you go along. Obviously, either you are currently in sales or you aren't. If you are a working salesman, take a product or service you are currently selling and apply each point to it as you go along. In other words, start right now to make the 20 Points improve your sales approach in the specific area of selling where you're most interested.

If you are a student of salesmanship and aren't currently employed as a salesman, select a product or service in an area that interests you—something you think you might like to sell. Pick a product or service where you can get complete information—not only about the item but about the company that sells it. If there is a sales manual available, get it. Stick to that chosen item as long as you can get the information you need. Should you reach a point where you are uninformed and can't dig up the facts you need, don't worry. Simply switch to a product or service on which the information is obtainable.

The idea of this book is to teach you how to apply the basic components of selling to anything you might ever be called upon to sell. You must learn how to apply the sales fundamentals before you can hope to do a good selling job on anything.

If you are working in a group or class, the group leader or instructor should direct both general and specific questions to members of the group and should try to work out an application of each point to the product or service being used for teaching purposes. Please don't get the idea that it's enough to understand the meaning of a point. You must know how to use that point and how to arrive at its best possible use in a specific instance.

Don't be afraid of coming up with approaches that seem either too far out or too conservative. Usually, most people start at one extreme or the other and finally arrive at the best use of the point. It's healthy to get the weak or unsound uses out into the open and tossed into the discard. Really, it's about the only way you can learn to recognize poor selling approaches.

It's always helpful to work with someone else so that you can actually go through your approach to a point orally. One person becomes the buyer and the other the seller. If you can do this on every point, you'll retain the basic idea of the point better.

If you can go through the Personal points with a stranger, so much the better. Get about as much information on him as you would normally have in a "cold turkey" selling situation. Then when you've done an oral rehearsal of a point, let him tell you what kind of an impression you made on him. A stranger will usually be more honest about it than a friend.

You'll See Yourself Progress

Building a sales presentation is fun. As you see it take shape, leaving nothing to chance, you should become excited about it. I'm assuming that you have a genuine respect for the profession of selling and realize that most of the top executives in this country are where they are because they've done an expert selling job of one kind or another.

You're improving yourself in the one profession where there's no limit to how high you can go. So let's get those 20 Points to you as simply and quickly as we can. We start with the Personal points, and you are about to learn something about them that is one of the great but often ignored truths of selling.

The Personal Elements

Heretofore, the opening of a sales solicitation has been called just that—the opening. And I suppose you can't argue much about such nomenclature without getting into some rather complex semantics.

But when we were putting together the Dartnell/Anderson 20-Point System for Guaranteed Sales Success, we realized that the first points —what had been called the opening—really had little to do with the product or service a man was selling. They depended on *him*, not his wares.

One of the great truths in selling is the statement, "Other things being equal, people buy from people they like." All selling has to start from that premise.

Of course, other things are seldom equal, but—other things being equal, people buy from people they like.

Why do we start with the personal element in selling? Well, contrary to what's often said, sales are not made to markets but to people. You seldom ever sell a business firm. You sell a person in that firm. And the flat statement that people prefer to buy from people they like is an indisputable fact, proven in every test of it that's ever been made.

Now, I'll grant you that other things are seldom equal. The opposition has a price advantage, or a particularly appealing new model. It must have something or it couldn't stay in business. Conceivably, the buyer has orders from his boss to patronize a certain firm because of a preference for it. There's nearly always an unbalancer of some kind, but—we have to start with the premise that the salesman's first job is to make the customer like him.

This doesn't mean that you become a soft-soap artist. Insincere flattery is usually both obvious and distasteful. It doesn't mean that you learn an assortment of parlor tricks or that you spend a lot of money on lavish entertaining.

How do you get the prospect to like you? There are a number of ways, but ask yourself this question: Who do people like? The answer's easy: People who like them, who show a genuine interest in them, who aren't completely submerged in their own selfish interests.

Man's first law is the law of self-preservation, and his second major interest is self-advancement. His own problems are his paramount concern, and he couldn't care less about yours—until he acquires a personal interest in you. Once he decides he likes you, you become a part—maybe a minor part but still a part—of his selfish interests.

Be Grateful to Customer

The late Will Rogers' statement, "I never met a man I didn't like," has been quoted at least often enough to last me for the rest of my lifetime. Let's face it, some people are pretty unattractive. I've met a few where liking them took considerable effort—until I developed this selling philosophy:

> *"I'm thankful to this man for giving me the time to tell my story. I'm grateful to him for the business favors he may grant me if I make the right approach. I like this man for the order he may place with me."*

From your own selfish standpoint, there's every reason to like your prospective customer. For one thing, your job becomes much pleasanter. And just as people preferably buy from people they like, you'll find it's far, far easier to *sell* people you like.

Some salesmen sell almost entirely on the personal points. They happen to be men with great personal charm of one kind or another, and they know how to turn that charm on with such strength that they almost hypnotize their prospects into buying.

When I was radio-television director of a large advertising agency,

I was called on constantly by salesmen for film studios who hoped to get the business of filming commercials for our clients. Most of them had the same sales pitch—the great creativity they would add to the commercial copy our agency turned out and to the filming of it. That creativity, they said, was what we were really paying for when we bought from them.

Creativity Wasn't Wanted

Now it so happened that on the major accounts we were handling, the clients didn't *want* any creativity. They knew exactly what they wanted to say and how they wanted their commercials made. What we showed to a film studio was it—nothing to be added and nothing to be taken away. One client in particular raised a real ruckus whenever a studio tried to improve the film, even going so far as to make them do the whole job over according to exact specifications.

There was always one film salesman I *wanted* to give assignments, although only occasionally was I able to do it. This one man sold his own personality. He made you feel that once you placed a job with his company, he would stand right over it to see that you got what you wanted, with no ifs, ands, or buts.

I still believe that this man *did* like me. He couldn't have conducted himself the way he did if he'd found me obnoxious. But I suspect that one good reason why he liked me was that I represented a potential source of business.

He was always on the lookout for some little, really unusual gift that he thought would particularly appeal to one of his potential customers. These gifts were never ostentatious things, but neither were they ever pointless. The gift always showed this salesman's knowledge of a prospect's interests.

When he heard a good joke, he didn't say, "That's a good story for me to tell my prospects." Rather, he said, "Hey, that's a story that will appeal to Bill Blank, because he was in a situation like that a few weeks ago."

The personal element in selling is much like the Attention Compeller in advertising. Long ago, advertising experts learned that they had to attract attention to their advertising if they hoped to have it read. Most of them learned that it must be *favorable* attention if they hoped to make sales from it.

Before we get to the personal points that influence sales, let's talk briefly about personality factors that influence salesmen.

Two problems, aside from not knowing their jobs, keep more salesmen from being successful than anything else.

The first is an apologetic attitude toward being a salesman. The economy of the world depends on salesmen. No matter how good a product or how good a company's advertising, the company's fate finally rests in the hands of salesmen.

And yet, many salesmen aren't proud of their jobs. They spend a good deal of time looking for "something better than being a peddler." They fight sales success every minute.

Management Realizes Importance

It certainly isn't that their immediate bosses feel that way about salesmen. And I've had chairmen of the boards of alert, successful corporations tell me that the salesman is actually the key man in their operations. "With a good sales force, we make money," one board chairman told me. "With a weak sales force, we lose our shirts. It's that simple."

The president of one company said, "I wish I knew how to raise the morale of our salesmen. We baby them to a point where it's ridiculous. But, dammit, too many of them don't want to be salesmen. I don't know how to whip it."

The other problem is—wives. I guess some wives would rather have their husbands get impressive titles than impressive money. And the wife who understands her salesman husband's job is a rare jewel.

When a salesman is good enough, he's going to be sent all over the world to close sales. "Traveling" is one of the dirtiest words in the dictionary to many wives.

A young man who was a real ball of fire as a salesman went into a selling slump three months after his marriage. His wife was outraged at the hours he put in and the amount of time he spent on the road. Life at home became miserable to the point where he finally told his sales manager his problem.

He was fortunate enough to have a sales manager who was sympathetic. The young fellow's plight stirred him to action, because he didn't want to lose such a bright and promising boy.

Set Up School for Wives

He set up a two-day indoctrination course for the wives of all his salesmen. Give him credit; he had nerve.

He told the wives in essence, "There are inconveniences in every job in the world. No position in this company or any company that I know anything about is all peaches and cream.

"On a great many jobs, I honestly think that the inconveniences outweigh the returns. With salesmen, I think quite the contrary. A salesman is *paid* for the inconvenience he suffers. You as a salesman's wife are paid for your inconveniences.

"The salesmen in this company have higher incomes than the people in any other department, even including research, where we have some bona-fide geniuses.

"Because your husband is a good salesman, you can have a higher standard of living than most people of your age and educational background. You also have job security that many wives don't have. Let business go into a slump, and many departments have to be closed down. But the good salesman becomes more important to the company. It's his efforts that can break the slump. He's needed, because his job determines the economic welfare of the company."

He did a rundown on every man's territory and showed those wives how hard their husbands had to hustle to cover their calls. "We could cut their territories in half," he said, "which would give them much more time at home. But of course, if we cut their territories in two, it becomes a simple matter of dollars and cents that we must cut their income in half, too."

He answered questions for three hours—and he learned that most of the wives were unhappy because they hadn't had the faintest idea of their husband's responsibilities and objectives.

What this sales manager did for his men, most salesmen must do for themselves—and can do if they'll just face up to it. Once a wife understands the facts of life about her husband's work, she becomes much easier to live with, and much more sympathetic.

Aside from knowledge, which is vital, a good salesman must have the two intangible factors that The Scientist sales manager stresses—enthusiasm and confidence. These must be part of his personality.

Knowledge Builds Confidence

Knowledge of the fundamentals of selling, properly applied to your product or service, can build confidence that you can't get in any other way. The pseudo-confidence displayed by some salesmen is pathetically apparent, with lack of know-how showing through it like a spotlight. You get real confidence from knowing that you're a pro. You get it when you prove to yourself that the most difficult sales assignments aren't too tough for you. Any shortcut to confidence is a delusion.

Enthusiasm is something else. It can be self-generated or induced from an outside source. When you begin to realize the potential you have in the sales field, enthusiasm should come on strong.

You undoubtedly have personal goals aside from business success. Once you see that your ability as a salesman can move you toward those goals, you have every reason to be enthusiastic about what you're doing on the job. It can be the means of getting you what you want out of life.

You need enthusiasm about the product or service you're selling. If you can't honestly generate that enthusiasm, it's improbable that you'll generate much enthusiasm for your wares in the people you try to sell. What you're selling and how well you sell it must be important to you before you can generate enthusiasm in other people. The man who tries to be enthusiastic about what he's selling and just can't make it should switch immediately to something else. He's wasting his time trying to sell somebody else when he can't sell himself, and he's doing both himself and the company he represents a grave disservice.

In my opinion, bringing any meritorious product or service to the people who need it is worthy of great enthusiasm. It's a fine job, a challenging job, and one with deep satisfactions.

Just for fun, I asked the six sales managers who helped me to prepare word pictures of an amateur salesman and a pro. Putting their composites together, we arrived at these:

A Typical Amateur Salesman

If you're a typical amateur salesman, you're embarrassed by the loud, flamboyant types who seem to be part of your profession.

You have to be nice to so many people on the job that you hope you won't meet anybody new after working hours.

You turn in a complete, detailed sales report on every call you make.

You feel that the one way to get ahead is to economize. You try to save as much money as you can.

Your tastes are simple.

You hope that your sales job will lead to something better, preferably an executive job in the office.

Your earnings range from $7,200 to $10,000. You'd like to earn more.

Your wife wishes you'd do something else. She feels that your work takes too much of your time.

You're cautious. When you see how some salesmen gamble, it makes you ill. You can't understand the luck that some happy-go-lucky salesmen seem to have.

You're loyal to your company. If you have any grievances, you know enough to keep them to yourself.

You work hard, and you feel that there must be an easier way to make a living.

You know there are other salesmen in the company selling a higher dollar volume of business, but you'd like to see them do it with the accounts that are on your list.

You hope that what your job eventually leads to will be worth the current unpleasantness it involves.

You think that if you make enough calls, you'll close orders—just on the law of averages.

A Typical Pro Salesman

If you're a typical pro salesman, you're an extrovert. You like people. Gregariousness is a way of life for you.

You don't like desk jobs. You don't like detail work. You prefer moving around to being inside.

You try to justify short sales reports by big orders.

You're free and easy with your money. Nobody can accuse you of being a tightwad.

You have expensive tastes, which you try to justify.

Your earnings range from $12,000 to $50,000 a year, depending more upon the firm you're with than your ability. Being with people you like and having an interesting challenge are actually more appealing to you than money—up to a point.

You love praise and try to deserve it.

You don't think the president of the company is one bit better than you are, and you don't envy him his job.

Your wife feels that your work takes too much of your interest and vitality. She may be a little bit jealous of your feeling for your job.

You're a gambler. You'll shoot the works on your convictions.

You're loyal to your company, but you howl to high heaven about grievances, some of which are real and some imaginary.

Your work is fun for you.

Humility is one attribute you don't have. You're cocky, because you know you're doing a good job.

You're hard to get along with when you're in a selling slump.

If you need more money for any reason, you get out and earn it.

If you feel you have a raise coming, you ask for it.

You know your job. And you don't want any help from anybody, if you can possibly avoid it.

Some of the salesmen whose personalities contributed to these composites were amateurs and some were pros. Do you recognize yourself in any of the personality traits in either composite?

Whether you do or not, once you really understand the personal points in selling, you'll know more about salesmanship than you've ever understood before. So let's get to the Personal points right away.

1. Did I make a favorable impression on the customer?

You've noticed that this first point is in the form of a question. You will finally use the 20 Points as a self-evaluation checklist, and the easiest way to use them at that time is in question form. Since we're trying to keep everything as simple and basic as possible, we keep the question form all the way through.

Note that the question isn't, "Did I sell him," but "Did I, as a salesman, make a favorable impression on him?"

This point involves making an opening that shows *immediate* interest in the customer. You can make some statement or ask some question that shows interest and understanding in a hurry. The right opening statement always makes an impression.

Always remember, people make snap judgments. Every man believes he's a superior judge of people. So the *first* impression you make conditions the customer.

Blend With Your Customers

One thing that plays a part in that first impression is your personal appearance. If you look like you can't afford to wear a clean shirt every day and keep your clothes pressed, you won't create much confidence.

On the other hand, I knew a salesman who was calling on plumbing and heating contractors with a line of furnaces. He dressed like he was trying out for the romantic lead in a Broadway play. Everything he wore was flashy. And every plumber he called on showed an almost immediate distrust.

It would seem to be so fundamental as not to be worth saying that a salesman should dress to fit in with the people he's selling, but there are glaring evidences every day of salesmen not doing it.

I had one salesman working for me when I was manager of The Chicago *Tribune* Newspaper Advertising service who liked to drive a Cadillac. He could afford to drive one and there was no real reason why he shouldn't have. But he always parked that car at least two blocks away from the newspaper where he was calling.

Cadillac Was Wrong Image

"I'm selling a service," he explained, "and nobody can set a fixed price on a service." If I drive up in front of the newspaper office in a Cadillac, my prospect's first thought may be, "That service must be over-priced if the salesman can afford a Cadillac."

Haircuts and shaves are a part of that first physical impression. Bleary, blood-shot eyes can be a mighty bad part of it. There are men to whom a fresh shoe-shine is almost a fetish. If someone with dirty shoes calls on them, they form an immediate bad opinion.

One of my salesmen was doing fairly well. A buyer in his territory came up to me at a convention and said, "George, there's something I've been wanting to ask you. Is that Fred Moogins who calls on me from your place a queer?"

Well, Fred certainly wasn't anything but masculine. So I asked this buyer whatever gave him his impression. "Every time he comes into my office," he answered, "the perfume smell likes to knock you on your tail. I open all the windows the minute he leaves. Man, I tell you, I'd be embarrassed to have anybody come into my office after he leaves until I get it aired out."

Fred, it turned out, liked his shaving lotion powerful. And he learned, when he switched to a much milder brand, what some others he called on had thought.

Did I make a favorable impression on the customer?

You can't do anything about your height or your face—but most of the physical aspects of the first impression are fairly simple to control.

What you say in opening, though, is something else again.

When I was a teen-age kid, I started out one summer to sell the Savage Ovenette, door to door. It was a good product—an oven you could put on a gas or electric burner. After five or six calls where I got a quick brush-off, the idea seeped through that I better start saying something to get the housewife's immediate attention.

Where Angels Fear to Tread

To the best of my recollection, I was a young fifteen. I rang the next doorbell and when the housewife, middle-aged, came to the door, I said politely, "How do you do. Would you like a little oven?" I've seen some startled women, but never any to top that gal. I looked properly shocked, and apologized. "Gee, I didn't realize how that would sound. I'm selling the Savage Ovenette—it's a little oven that sits right on top of the stove. You can bake potatoes in it or biscuits or even a pie, without going to all the trouble of heating up the oven. I'm so embarrassed I hardly know how to apologize—but I'll bet you would like a little (pause) Savage Oven, at that."

I'd hardly recommend the approach to any adult salesman, but I sold Ovenettes at eight straight houses before a mean-faced woman told me I was a little smart-alec.

One friend, a top salesman who's a Southerner, always does the same thing on any first call. He says, "I wish you luck, sir. I always give every man who gives me an appointment one of these little ol' black-eyed peas. Carry it with your change, and it will bring you luck."

Derek Alberts has an opening on big, important sales calls that's so blatant I'd never be able to use it—but it works for him. He says, "Pardon me, sir, but I've heard so much about you and how important you are in the industry that I'm kind of nervous now that I've gotten in to see you." Most of the really big, important men I've ever run across will do more to put you at ease than the little fellows, so the psychology behind the approach is sound.

33

Advertisers test copy, and the headline to an ad can be compared to the opening in a sales presentation. Changing a weak headline to a strong one tripled sales for one advertiser. Maybe changing your opening approach can do as much for you.

In some cases, a personal question that shows your interest in the customer may be the right opening approach. When you get a prospective customer to talk about his own interests or even his hobbies while you listen attentively, he has to like you.

The greatest salesman I've ever known in my life told me something about the personal aspect of selling that I've never forgotten. He said, "When you show that you think a customer is a smart person, he's absolutely handcuffed in one respect—he *cannot* think you're stupid. Your judgment of him has ruled out that possibility."

I once wrote a little book for International Harvester salesmen that really covered only one point in selling, the salesman's personal attitude, and how it affects the prospect's attitude. If, in your approach, you take the mental attitude, "I want to sell you something," you create immediate resistance. If you take the mental attitude, "I want to help you buy something," you get favorable attention.

Think it over. Two salesmen on a retail floor approach you. One asks, "Did you want something?" The other says, "I'd like to help you if I may," and makes a favorable impression.

Each Impression a New One

In a seminar I conducted, a bright salesman came up with this: "What you're talking about in Point 1 is first calls—calls on strangers. But I've already made a first impression on most of the people I call on." And the answer is, "Not so." Every time you walk into a man's office, he gets a first impression of you. It's much easier, of course, to make a good opening impression on a man you already know. It's so easy, in fact, that many salesmen don't even bother trying to make *any* impression. They take it for granted that a relationship has already been established.

Did I make a favorable impression on the customer?

The professional salesman knows how he's going to open every time he begins a sales solicitation. And he opens with something that he thinks will make a strongly favorable personal impression.

Obviously, I don't know what you're selling. But ask yourself, "What would be the best thing I could possibly say to this particular prospect to make a good impression on him?"

Some salesmen try hard to get quick attention, without considering whether or not the attention is favorable.

Avoid the Off-Color Story

I once had a salesman working for me who fancied himself as a story teller. He always had a few new stories and got laughs with them. But his stories ranged from slightly off-color to downright filthy. He told dirty stories to new prospects. Finally, some of his prospects who happened to know me told me that they found him objectionable because of his latrine humor.

Greg was mystified when I told him about it. "But they all laughed," he protested. "They laughed hard at my stories."

Men who dislike dirty stories *often* laugh at them. They feel that they're supposed to laugh and that failure to react somehow establishes them as effeminate.

I know many men who enjoy off-color humor—but I doubt if I know anybody who respects a stranger who tells him dirty jokes.

When I first did lecture dates for the W. Colston Leigh Bureau, I was told by the bureau management, "One thing we will not tolerate is the use of dirty stories. When you're playing a stag date, the program chairman may even tell you that he hopes you'll have some good, racy, red-blooded stories. Pay no attention to him. If you do tell off-color stories, we'll get a letter of protest from somebody in the group. It never fails."

Mannerisms sometimes make an unfavorable impression on a cus-

35

tomer. Since they're quite often habit, a salesman can annoy a prospect without realizing why.

I remember a television network sales manager who was always at ease in any situation. And I remember how he lost a major sale. He was in the office of a multimillionaire president of a company and he tilted his chair back as he talked. He balanced it as skillfully as any professional acrobat could. And to keep the chair from falling back forward, he had the soles of his shoes against the front of his prospect's priceless antique desk.

The prospect was so annoyed that he scarcely heard anything the network sales manager said. He told me later that he had been fascinated in a morbid way. "I kept hoping he'd fall and hurt himself," he confessed.

One time I made a call with a salesman who "washed his hands" throughout the solicitation. All the time he talked, he rubbed his hands together, over and under each other. When the call was ended, I stepped back into the customer's office and asked him privately if the mannerism had annoyed him. "Annoy?" he said. "It darned near drove me crazy."

One salesman I know is a chronic doodler. He doesn't even know he's doing it. And some of his doodles are works of art. They're so interesting, in fact, that they quite often overshadow the sales message.

Upstaged By a Diamond Ring

Jerry Lewis, the comedian, was asked one time as a favor to watch and criticize a friend's new act, and he agreed to do it.

"Well, how did you like the new act?" the friend asked anxiously at the conclusion of the performance.

"I'll be honest with you," Jerry answered. "I never quite got around to watching your act."

Did I make a favorable impression on the customer?

"What do you mean by a crazy statement like that?" the friend asked.

"Well," Jerry said, "you had that huge diamond ring on your left hand, and the lights caught it pretty good. Between the ring and the lemon-colored slacks and light blue jacket you were wearing, you had my attention so strongly that I never got past them."

The performer had dressed that way to attract attention—but it had been the wrong kind of attention, directed to the wrong area. Salesmen sometimes make the same mistake.

One thing that's seldom discussed about personal impressions is voice level, but don't ever get the idea that it isn't important.

Neither Mumble Nor Boom and Bellow

There's a salesman who calls on me who I've secretly nicknamed "Mumbles." By the time he leaves, I've worn myself out trying to hear what he's mumbled. I can't say I've been much impressed. Too low a voice creates an impression that you're frightened or insecure. The only attention it commands is sympathy for an affliction.

Another salesman is the direct opposite. He comes into my office and with only two of us there uses a stage voice adequate for an audience of a thousand people. He booms and bellows. I never hear him without the phrase, "A big bag of wind," entering my mind.

There's a happy medium which is admittedly hard to find without some coaching from another person. To make a good impression, you speak clearly, firmly and directly, in a voice that can be heard without straining but never assails the eardrums. It's been interesting to me to note that the salesman who uses this voice level is usually well-informed. He has the situation in hand, right from the start. When a salesman either mumbles or shouts, I always have the feeling that he doesn't know quite as much as he should about his sales solicitation and that lack of confidence in himself is responsible for the voice level difficulty.

20-Point System for Guaranteed Sales Success

Tricks to make a quick impression on a customer are numerous, but most of them aren't very good and quite a few of them are downright bad. The trouble is that they're usually recognizable as tricks, and prospective customers distrust trickery. My personal feeling is that you can't blame them. With an honest effort to make a good impression, you don't need tricks.

Some of the best ways to make a favorable impression are:

Opening remarks slanted to the customer's interests.

Personal approach—both clothes and grooming.

Voice level—firm and distinct, but not overpowering.

Good manners without annoying mannerisms.

A show of respect and liking for the customer.

A general deportment that reflects competence.

If you have these things, you won't need to worry about vaudeville tricks to capture the prospect's interest.

The first impression you make on the customer can get you off to a flying start. It's possible to overcome a bad first impression, but it takes time and work—and why should any salesman handicap himself when it isn't necessary?

Some Starter Questions on Point 1

Here are some starter questions to get you thinking about Point 1.

1. Do you have any mannerisms that you think might possibly be irritating to people?

2. In your opinion, what would be proper dress for a salesman calling on small-town retail merchants? City professional men? How would you dress if you were an automobile salesman? What do you think would be proper attire for the item or service you're selling?

3. How do you feel you could best show a prospective buyer that you like him, without being obviously flattering?

Did I make a favorable impression on the customer?

4. Do you think your conversational voice level is good or bad?

5. What opening remarks do you make now? Do they do the things they should do?

Remember this. When you ask yourself at the conclusion of a sales solicitation, "Did I make a favorable impression on the customer?" and your answer is "No," you don't have to look any further to know why you didn't make a sale.

2. Did I talk
from the customer's
viewpoint?

At the start of a sales presentation, the customer's and your interests are usually a mile apart.

The customer isn't even mildly interested in your making a sale. He's interested in himself and what benefit you might possibly be to him. When a customer says, "I'm buying this to help you," I simply don't believe him.

When you show eagerness to make a sale, you're on dangerous ground, not working from the customer's viewpoint. Too apparent eagerness to close a sale has built up resistance in many a buyer— as I well know.

Let me confess right here that inability to submerge my eagerness to close has always been a problem for me. I have to fight it every time I make a call. I *am* eager, and when I let my eagerness show through too much and too quickly, I know I make my job more difficult.

They Don't Really Care About You

A salesman once told me that he said to a chain-store buyer, "Selling you will mean so much to our company that we'll give you absolutely perfect service." And the buyer replied, "I don't give a damn what selling our group will mean to your company—and I expect perfect service from *any*body who sells me."

The approach that, "We're having a sales contest and if you'll just

Did I talk from the customer's viewpoint?

give me this order today, it will help me win a free trip to Bermuda," is undoubtedly one of the worst ever made.

That's not talking from the customer's viewpoint but strictly from yours.

It's hard to believe but I once heard a salesman say, "If I don't get out of here by 3 o'clock, I'll miss my plane and will have to stay overnight, so let's get down to the order fast."

The key word is "you," not "I." And you try to talk the customer's language, using words he or she will understand. If you're selling a car to a housewife, you probably don't talk about torque or high compression.

Talk on the Customer's Level

This doesn't mean that you talk down to a customer or use double negatives if a customer does, any more than it means you use profanity because a customer swears. It means you talk in terms a customer will understand.

My friend McCorkle was the best furniture salesman I ever ran across. No customer was too small for Mac to give anything but his best sales efforts, and no customer was large enough to awe him.

I watched him work one afternoon when a railroad section hand and his wife came into the store. Their English wasn't too good, and probably their credit wasn't, either.

Mac said, "Now, I don't want to load you with a lot of expensive things you don't need or don't want. I'd like to plan how you can spend your furniture money to the best advantage. To do that, I should know how much money you can spend, right now." The woman opened a bag and counted out close to $700.

Mac did a conscientious job of finding them good values, and he was getting along fine until it came to buying a living room set. Absolutely nothing on the floor appealed to them—and I mean nothing, at any price.

Mac snapped his fingers and said, "I've got it! Just the thing for you. Stay right here while I bring it down and show it to you." He got into the freight elevator and went up to the storage room, where he hauled out a davenport and easy chair with a batik sunburst across the back of each piece. The colors were easily the most violent I've ever seen. He shoved the set onto the freight elevator and brought it down to the first floor, where he rolled it off.

"Well," he said, almost reverently, "there she is. Just the set for you! Ain't that a bitch?" They nodded enthusiastically and said, "We take."

Mac had the customer's viewpoint.

A friend of mine in the rebuilt machinery business told me of a mistake his competitor made. Both firms had heard that the XYZ Company wanted to change its production setup but couldn't afford to buy new machinery.

My friend's competitor went in with recommendations and a perfectly sound, truthful story of how installation of the equipment he offered could double production while increasing production cost only 14%.

My friend went in and showed the XYZ people how they could cut production costs 15% on the number of units they were currently turning out. He got the order.

What the Customer Really Wanted

"You see," he explained, "my competitor hadn't bothered to find out what it was all about. The XYZ Company had slipped badly and their heavy equipment was too cumbersome to operate for the volume of units they could sell. They had no desire whatsoever to increase production. They simply wanted to cut production cost on the volume they were doing."

He took the trouble to learn the customer's viewpoint and talk with it in mind.

Did I talk from the customer's viewpoint?

Sometimes the customer's viewpoint can be tricky. I once made a million-dollar sale by saying, "We've checked with legal counsel and it's perfectly legitimate for you to pay for this now and use it next year." I'd learned that this particular prospect had a rather complex tax problem which completely reversed his customary viewpoint.

Goals have a great deal to do with viewpoints. Do you know what each of your prospective customers is trying to do? And don't answer, "Make money." It's not that simple. You may be talking to people who are milking a company for every dime they can take out of it, or you may be talking to a growth company that wants to keep dividends low and expansion high. Does the customer find what you're selling a luxury or a necessity? You'd better find out and talk accordingly.

Does he want an immediate return from what you're trying to sell him or is he looking at the long haul?

Get Involved With Customer's Business

A good example of customer viewpoint is a slidefilm I once did for the Staley Company of Decatur, Illinois.

Bakeries were a logical market for corn syrup. Staley Sweetose could do a wonderful job for any bakery of almost any size. And yet, in all the years the Staley Company had been selling syrup, they'd put in only 15 bakery installations.

When I asked why, I was told, "You can't sell them. You can't get past the purchasing agent. A bakery installation will run from $12,000 to $15,000 before they can use the syrup—and to make that sale, you have to get the bakery owner, the plant foreman or manager, the advertising manager, and the sales manager together—along with the purchasing agent."

We prepared a baking clinic on slidefilm, calling it "Unsliced Profits." It really showed the bakery how it could improve its product while drastically cutting materials-handling costs. We showed how the bakery could increase the shelf life of its bread, cutting down on

43

returns that ruin profits. Practically the entire film was devoted to the bakery's viewpoint, not the Staley Company's.

The Staley salesmen had a training session in which they were instructed not to show the film to the purchasing agent. The entire group had to be assembled.

And what happened? The same sales force that had sold a dozen or so installations in a long period of years sold some 20 installations in the next 60 days.

It was a matter of talking from the customer's viewpoint.

One of the highest compliments a prospective customer can pay to a salesman is to say, "You must have been in this business at some time or another." Of course, what he is really saying is, "Fella, you sure know how to talk from my viewpoint."

How to Get the Right Answers

In a seminar, when one of the salesmen protested, "But how do you find the customer's viewpoint?" another man jumped to his feet and said, "It's easy."

"Yeah?" the first salesman said. "I suppose you know just what to say."

"I sure do," the second salesman acknowledged.

"Where did you learn how to read minds?"

"You don't have to read minds, wise guy, and you don't have to guess," Salesman No. 2 insisted. "I simply get the right answers while I'm waiting."

"Waiting for what?"

"Waiting to get in to see and talk to the prospect. I'm either with a receptionist or a secretary until I can get into the man's office. And if you want to know about a prospect, you can't find two better people to question. Either one of them can tell you more about the guy than

Did I talk from the customer's viewpoint?

he knows about himself. They'll give you his hobbies, his eccentricities, his pet peeves—real prejudices, sometimes—his enthusiasms, the inside dope on his sex life—you name it and they can tell you for real."

"Maybe," the first salesman said, "you run into receptionists and secretaries who blab everything they know—but there are some who are too smart to talk to salesmen."

"Sure," the second salesman agreed. "And when I find one of those, I still make my waiting time pay dividends."

"How?"

Clues in the Reception Room

"I read all the literature that's on display. First, I grab the house organ. You can get information from it that you won't find anywhere else. Company attitudes are reflected in it. I've never looked at a piece of printing in a reception room that didn't help me in some way to learn the viewpoint of the fellow I'm waiting to see. If I can't get the girl to talk. I grab the company literature and start reading. At the least, I have an approach to the prospect's viewpoint before I get into his office. In some cases, I've had an item in a house organ completely change my approach."

"For example—" Salesman No. 1 pressed.

"Well," No. 2 said, "if I read in the house organ that the company is on an expansion kick, with pressure being put on every employee to get things rolling, I'll certainly have a different sales presentation from the one I'll use if the house organ indicates there's a hammer-and-tongs summer economy drive."

He was so right. If you have to wait to see a prospect—which isn't at all unusual in spite of the best appointment planning—there's no better place to get a good line on your man than right there in his own place of business.

I recall soliciting an advertising account, and I had to wait. So I went back and talked a foreman into letting me look over the production line. On that line, I saw quality control that was unbelievably good. No other company in the same line had quality control that even came close.

As a result, my whole approach to the prospect was changed. He was too close to his quality control to realize what a weapon it could be for him in the company's advertising. When I pointed it out to him, he was quick to agree.

A salesman who was selling materials-handling equipment was forced to wait to talk to the purchasing agent. While waiting, he sauntered back and introduced himself to the plant foreman. The foreman welcomed him with open arms, because the poor fellow was under fire for his high materials-handling costs. What the salesman learned from the plant foreman showed him that his planned approach was all wrong. And with the company's viewpoint replacing his own, he was able to get a $100,000 order.

To close a sale, you must maneuver yourself onto common ground with the customer. Since he's never going to take your viewpoint, the only sensible thing to do is head straight for his.

A Self-Examination on Point 2

Here are a few "starter" questions in building your approach to Point 2, "Did I talk from the customer's viewpoint?"

1. How can I learn the customer's viewpoint?

2. How should I talk, to talk language that the customer understands and likes? What would be the right way to phrase my opening to talk the average customer's language?

3. How can I convey to the customer quickly that I'm sympathetic to his problems and interests?

4. How do I start talking about my product or service without giving the customer the idea that I'm too eager to close the sale in a hurry?

Did I talk from the customer's viewpoint?

5. What are all the things I need to know about the customer's viewpoint when I start talking to him?

Let's try a simple little mental exercise. You have learned that the customer's viewpoint is that he's grossly overworked. He apologizes to you for being so busy and says that you'll have to make your pitch fast, because he simply doesn't have much time. How do you show your empathy with him in such a situation?

3. Did I find the strongest desire or need of the customer and then capitalize on it?

Many a big sale has been made on this point alone. It's the obvious, even trite admonition to sell benefits, not goods.

Before you get anywhere with Point 3, you must give your product or service careful analysis. What benefits does it offer? What needs can it fill?

You'll probably wind up with a fair-sized list. Now, your next step is to translate those benefits and needs into buying urges.

Then comes the big step. What is the most important buying urge for the specific customer you want to sell? Is it Personal Importance or Prestige? Is it Health? Self-Preservation? Sex Urge? Convenience? Utility? Is it Economy?

Every first-rate salesman knows how to translate what he's selling into benefits—but not so many will take the trouble to find the benefit that can push the sale button on a particular call and then ride that benefit for all it's worth.

Obviously, it's always easier to sell somebody something he wants than something he *doesn't* want. So as quickly as you can, you translate your product or service into a specific customer's most wanted benefit.

What are the most effective appeals, generally speaking? Personal importance or prestige is sometimes important. A Tiffany label on a jewelry package is worth more than one from Joe's Cut-Rate Jewelry Store. Today, it's my firm conviction that at least half of the cars sold in this country are sold on this appeal. Cadillac, Imperial, Mercedes-Benz, Rolls, and similar names are regarded by some people as caste marks. Many women will gladly fork over extra dollars for a "Mr. John" label in a hat.

"A title on the door rates a Bigelow on the floor" sells personal importance. So does "Ask the man who owns one," as does "You just know she wears them."

Many a man pays a substantial initiation fee, plus monthly dues in perpetuity, to a private club for the privilege of buying lunches that aren't quite as good as he could get in a first-class restaurant. Along the same line, numerous restaurants have installed private eating clubs to get patrons who want personal importance and are willing to pay for it. The food often comes from the same kitchen.

The Cult of Countess Mara

When I was doing a series of lecture dates, I happened to wear a Countess Mara necktie (a gift, I might add) one night and found that there was almost a cult of Countess Mara tie wearers. And I learned that many wives were even more impressed by the CM design on a tie than were their husbands.

Why is personal importance so strong an appeal? Well, we all spend more money for things that aren't absolute necessities than for things that are. And when we buy luxuries, we want them to be as luxurious as possible. We want to show that we've Arrived.

Sex is certainly one of the strongest appeals—and in this instance, sex doesn't mean an overdeveloped Hollywood movie starlet. It may mean improved personal appearance, benefit to family, approval from the buyer's husband or wife—many things.

Hugh Hefner found that sex was a powerful benefit to offer, and he parlayed it into an empire.

Some time, some woman may have paid $25 an ounce for perfume because she liked the smell of it—but I doubt it. Do you know of any perfume advertising that emphasizes the product's delightful odor? I don't.

Even soap manufacturers resort to sex as a benefit that will create sales. Try to think of a sexier benefit than that offered by a soap to give "the skin you love to touch."

In cosmetics, the word "sex" changes to glamour or beauty—and the approaches to it are so outlandish as to be completely unbelievable to a male. Or *are they?* The sale of men's cosmetics goes up and up.

Convenience is sometimes a magic appeal. "Quick" and "Easy" are benefits that have overcome high prices many times. People like to do things the easy way, not the hard way.

The convenience appeal has almost revolutionized the food business. Prepared mixes, which almost invariably cost more, have skyrocketed in sales. "Instant" has become a real selling word to the housewife. Packaged frozen dinners aren't cheap—but they're easy to prepare and they sell for that reason. Frozen foods that you prepare without even removing from the package sell well; how can you get more convenience than that?

But convenience can go far beyond these examples. One manufacturer sells a lot of goods because he fills orders from six strategically located distribution centers, whereas his chief competitor ships everything from one factory. It's more convenient and quicker to order from the first company, and that's a definite benefit on a high-priced item when a dealer doesn't want a lot of money tied up in inventory.

Self-Preservation a Good Appeal

If anyone had told me in the early days of television that you could charge a stiff premium for adding a gadget that would permit you to tune a TV set from your chair without getting up and twisting the dial, I'd have said he was crazy. But the convenience appeal worked and is still working.

You'll find the phrase, "Convenient Location," in so many ads that it must do something for advertisers who use it.

Self-preservation is a powerful appeal. It accounts for the preval-

Did I find the strongest desire or need of the customer?

ence of so-called "scare" advertising. People will often buy because they're afraid not to. "I'm giving you first chance at this" is polite scare selling. What it says is, "If you don't take on this line, I'm going to your competitor with it."

Apparently, scare advertising can't be too crude to work. Will your loved ones have an income when you're no longer here? Don't be half-safe. Even your best friends won't tell you. Nobody loves a man with messy hair. B.O. Ba-a-a-d Breath. In more subtle forms of the self-preservation benefit, the wording is positive rather than negative, with the "scare" covered by implication. But the scare is still there.

Economy and Improvement Benefits

Economy is a basic benefit. Every buyer wants to buy advantageously, and when you show a customer how to save his money, he has to show some interest. The success of discount outlets all over the country is proof that the lure of economy is potent.

"Special Offer" used to be the strong economy lure. Today, it's apparently the "8 cents Off" coupon, and whether the coupon is for 5 cents or 50 cents, it pulls results.

"Large Economy Size" has increased sales for many a manufacturer, even though sometimes quick figuring will show you that it isn't really economical.

Improvement is a standard benefit, as the rash of use of the words "New and Improved" in advertising bears out. Sometimes about the only thing new or improved is the wording on the label, but the words seem to get results, even so.

Sometimes the most trivial benefits make the difference *when* those minor benefits happen to hit the right customer at the right time. A friend of mine bought an $800 outboard motor in preference to a lower-priced make because he liked the color combination.

Whatever you're selling, it has numerous buyer benefits. If it didn't have, it wouldn't stay on the market. Your first job under Point 3 is to determine *all* the buyer benefits of your product or service. Know them, and know how to state them in terms of great appeal. Then, when you find a prospective customer's major area of interest, you're ready to transform whatever you're selling into what he wants.

But how do you learn the benefit that's most important to a specific customer?

Mostly, you try to involve the customer in discussing what is desirable and what isn't in the kind of product or service you're selling. Then you watch and listen.

On occasion, I've found a blunt, direct approach the best solution to the problem, particularly when dealing with one of the Strong, Silent Types. I simply ask the man what he thinks is most important in a product of this kind, and why. The "and why" is important, because it sometimes shows that he's given an answer just to field the question and doesn't really think the thing he mentioned is important at all.

A Printed List of Benefits

Another approach I've used with the customer who won't express himself is to have the whole list of benefits printed in ink on a small card.

"The company's planning a new advertising campaign," I say, "and there's considerable argument about which benefit should be featured in the ad headline. There's plenty we can say about all the benefits listed on the card, but one of them has to be more important to potential customers than any other. So we're asking people we call on to help us out. Which of these features would you put in the headline? Why?"

The customer isn't as wary of this approach as the straight, direct question—and he likes the idea of being asked for advice on advertising.

When you have to ask, or have to use a trick approach, the solicita-

Did I find the strongest desire or need of the customer?

tion isn't going as well as it should. The prospect hasn't been participating or you'd already have your answer. Difficulty in learning the most important benefit is nearly always a warning signal to get the man more involved in the presentation.

We were discussing the problem in a sales meeting one time, and one of the salesmen said, "When a customer won't tell me what he wants, I just remind myself that you can't sell 'em all."

The sales manager jumped to his feet. "It's quite true that you can't sell 'em all," he agreed, "but let me tell you something. In this organization, you better darned well *try* to sell 'em all."

Don't Outguess Yourself!

To try to sell anybody anything, you need to know what the most effective appeal is for that man. Without knowing, you're shooting arrows into the air instead of aiming a rifle at a bull's-eye.

Let's assume that you're calling on a purchasing agent who is a big, heavy, easygoing fellow. You get the immediate impression that he's good-natured and that he'll give you all the time you want. He's better-dressed than most of the purchasing agents you meet.

What would your first guess be as to the benefit that will be most appealing to this fellow? Would it be convenience or comfort? Possibly. From the way he dresses, do you get the idea that perhaps personal importance or prestige might be the bell-ringer? That sounds good, too.

With what you're selling, how would you go about learning which of these two appeals would hit him harder? To make sure that you've gotten on the right track, what questions would you ask him? What other benefits would you mention to double-check that you're right?

Once you think you're right, how would you capitalize on your knowledge? How would you make the right benefit do a selling job for you?

Suppose you're calling on the president of a small company. His suit is good, but the fabric's shiny. His shoes are worn down at the heels. You get the feeling that he's under pressure, but you don't know what kind. He's nervous, and you don't think he'll give you much time. There's a plaque on his wall, an award from the Safety Council.

What benefits do you feel would appeal most to this man? How do you find out whether or not you're right? You better work fast on this fellow or you're going to lose him.

Well, I called on just such a man and my analysis was that economy would be the most appealing benefit. Every check seemed to prove that I was right, and I based the major appeal on economy. I made the sale—and then discovered later that this man was a multimillionaire. Had I known that when I entered his office, I'd have probably dismissed economy as a major benefit without even getting into it—and I'd have been completely wrong. Economy, it turned out, was a fetish with the fellow. His whole business success was based on it.

When you're checking your salesmanship, always ask yourself this question. "Did I find the strongest desire or need on the part of the customer and then capitalize on it?"

There have been sales courses that confined themselves almost exclusively to elaboration of this one point—and the courses weren't without value because you only complete a sale when somebody wants or needs what you're selling—or thinks he does.

Try These Questions on Point 3

For starter questions, try these.

1. If a prospect expresses great interest in the efficiency and proven rating of your product, what benefit should you stress? How do you work into that benefit from his questions about efficiency?

2. The customer has an oil portrait of himself on his office wall. How do you talk benefit to him?

3. The man excuses himself and takes two vitamin pills while you're talking to him. What benefit do you stress, and how do you go about it?

Did I find the strongest desire or need of the customer?

4. The prospect tells you flatly that the only thing he's interested in is price—that if you're lower than your competitors, you'll get the order. Actually, your initial purchase price is higher than competition's. What benefit do you try to sell to this man?

5. The customer says, "You have a beautiful piece of machinery there, and in theory it should save me money—but I'm a hard-headed guy. I have to be practical." What is your approach?

4. Did I encourage the customer to do part of the talking?

Nobody loves a big blabbermouth, and the most disliked salesman is the one who talks too much. He not only talks too much but he doesn't listen at all.

A sale is completed by a seller and a buyer, and *both* must participate.

One of the reasons I dislike being on the receiving end of so-called "canned" solicitations is that they seldom give me a chance to interrupt—which I always want to do.

I remember the time when I wanted to buy an educational endowment policy for my newborn son. I told an insurance man what I wanted and invited him to come to see me.

"Fine," I greeted him. "I want this to start paying off at age 18, a thousand dollars a year. What will that kind of a policy cost me?"

"Well," he said, "first, here's something I want to show you. Here you see the happy young couple with the new baby." He'd set up one of those damned canned presentations!

"Look," I interrupted, "I have a lot of work to turn out here at home tonight and I'm in a hurry. I know you represent a good company. What's the policy going to cost me?"

"We'll get to that," he said. "But first, here are the father and mother figuring out how they'll pay for the baby's education. They're trying to determine how much a week they can save for that purpose."

"Do you *have* to go through that thing?" I pleaded.

Did I encourage the customer to talk?

"As a matter of fact," he replied, "the company says this is the right way to do it."

"Far be it from me to get you in bad with your company," I answered. "So you go right ahead and go through the whole blankety-blank thing from start to finish. Meanwhile, I'm going into my den and get to work. When you're all through with that flip-over, call me and I'll come back out here into the living room and we can get down to business." I left the room.

The fellow looked at my wife. "I never had anything like this happen before," he said. "Won't he come back out and go through this with me?"

Mrs. Anderson Gives Odds

"I'd give you ten to one that he won't," my wife answered. "If I were you, I'd just *pretend* I'd gone through it and call him back out here and answer his questions."

The booklet that accompanied the canned solicitation had covered a number of contingencies—but not this one. He decided to follow my wife's advice, called me back into the room, answered my questions, and took my application for the policy, along with a check.

"Now, see how simple that was?" I asked. "Why were you so determined to go through that thing?"

"The company says it's the only way to do it," he insisted. "They say more of these policies are sold that way than any other."

"How has it been working out for you?" I asked.

"Well," he admitted, "not very good."

It's quite true that in some selling situations, a salesman must take charge, must dominate the conversation completely to get his story across. Professional purchasing agents often limit a salesman's selling time.

But it's equally true that many salesmen make their job far more difficult than need be by an almost appalling flow of words. On rare occasions, with really bad offenders, I've taken along one of those miniature recorders with tie-pin microphone. And the guilty salesmen have been aghast when they've heard the playback. Usually, these monologues get slightly incoherent in spots. You get the feeling that the salesman is scared to *let* the prospect say anything and that he'd rather prattle than listen.

It's sad, because you don't make a sale without letting the customer do some of the talking. You know from experience that the deadpan silent type is the most difficult to sell, because you can't deal with objections until they're out in the open.

Under Point 4, you think of things early in the sales presentation that will encourage *agreement*. If you tell a man you think he should be making more money, for example, he'll find it hard to disagree.

And after a customer has given you a "Yes" to a dozen little things, he's conditioned to say that same "Yes" with less difficulty when you finally ask for the order. But don't limit the customer's conversation to "yes" or "no." Only by getting him to talk will you find his problems and learn the benefits he's after.

The Man Who Talked Too Much

I mentioned to an executive that Joe Jason was a nice fellow. "I guess so," the man replied, "but every time he comes in here, he talks too damned much." And he added something I hadn't thought about until then. "He's damned discourteous," he said. "I invite him in here to talk about my needs in his field—to *discuss* those things. I'm entitled to at least tell him what I want him to talk about, but he doesn't let me. When I try to let him know what he needs to know to sell me, he interrupts me. And if he *does* let me get out a whole sentence, he doesn't hear a word I say. He's thinking of what *he's* going to say next."

Regardless of what you're selling, remember that your first objective is to make the prospect like you—to make a friend of him. And one of the obligations of friendship is to be a good listener. In selling, it's almost the only way to get certain information.

Did I encourage the customer to talk?

A pat sales presentation is usually too pat. The good salesman isn't a preacher; he's a conversationalist.

If you have to hire salesmen, you know that one good way to make up your mind on a man's potentiality is to *visit* with him. If he's a good visitor, he probably has the makings of a good salesman. If he wants to talk about himself to the exclusion of almost everything else, pass him by. He won't make it.

Good Listeners Learn More

When you ask yourself, "Did I encourage the customer to do part of the talking?," ask yourself two subquestions:

1. Did I listen?

2. Did I profit from what I heard?

And bear this truth in mind: you always *learn* more from listening than you do from talking.

A young salesman just out of college made his youth and inexperience pay off for him. On every call, early in his solicitation, he said, "I probably don't need to tell you that I'm new on this job. On the first few calls I've made, I've already learned quite a few things they didn't teach me at the office. I know that you're an important man in this field and that you've had a lot more experience than anybody I've called on so far.

"If you were in my place, as inexperienced as I am and calling on men who have a great deal of experience, what would you talk about first in your presentation? How would you start?"

Believe me, this boy had a self-starter question. Every time he used it, he got the customer to do a large part of his selling job for him. There aren't many men who can resist telling a salesman how to sell, particularly when that salesman has asked for help—and must be an exceptionally bright young man, because he's come to such an excellent source.

If course, for an old pro to use this device would be the most blatant, obvious attempt at flattery. It wouldn't be believable.

Most good pro salesmen have four or five "starter" questions—provocative questions that spur a man into expressing his opinion. And the subject always happens to be something that fits right in with the pro's sales solicitation.

For example, one of them said to a customer, "I have an interesting question for you. If you were to buy out your No. 1 competitor and somebody tried to stop you on a charge that you were building a monopoly, what would you do?"

The man talked loud and clear, expressing his opinion of regulation and interference. When he finally subsided, the salesman said, "The reason I ask is that we're being accused of having a monopoly in our field, although we actually have a good many competitors. But how did our company get to its present leadership? We did it by constantly improving our products and offering our customers better value than they could get anywhere else. We've just made another improvement which is a dandy. So far, it's exclusive—but we know that in a few months, some of our competitors will start demanding that we license them to use it. I don't think that's fair—but meanwhile, they don't have it and we do. And I think you'll agree that it's great."

After demonstrating the exclusive feature, the salesman then asked, "If you had developed this and had it all to yourself, how would you go about keeping your competitors from eventually getting it? Or would you license them to use it right now?"

The Customer Takes the Bait

The customer said, "I'd license them right now. They'll have to pay you for every one they sell, so you'll be making money on their sales as well as your own. And you can undersell them, because your company won't have any licensing fee to figure into the cost."

"Say," the salesman said, "I never thought of that. I'm going to use your name, if you don't mind, when I point this out at the office."

One salesman told me, "I always get the customer talking right at the outset of my call. I have a surefire way of doing it. Before I get

Did I encourage the customer to talk?

into his office, I ask his secretary about his children, no matter how old or young they are. And as quickly as I can, I ask *him* about his kids. That opens him up, and getting him to continue to talk as the sales presentation progresses is easy."

All you have to do to convince yourself of the importance of Point 4 is to run up against a customer who simply won't talk. He sits back and looks at you, completely deadpan. And if there is a harder man to sell in the world, I've never found him. It's hard work to even get him to nod agreement on something you've just tried to establish. As far as getting him to say "Yes" is concerned, forget it. He isn't going to commit himself 'til you ask for the order. And that is sometimes the one way you can get this fellow to talk—ask for the order.

How One Salesman Handles It

The Old Timer, one of the sales managers who helped to build the 20-Point System, says that when he runs into such a customer, he asks for the order almost immediately. The prospect says, "No."

"So," this sales manager says, "I ask him why? One of them answered me last week, 'Why, you damn fool, you haven't told me anything about it yet. You haven't even given me one reason why I should buy.' And I said, 'Joe, I apologize. I assumed that you knew as much about this as I do. Exactly what is it you'd like to know before you make up your mind?' That got him started."

You will also run into the opposite of the Strong, Silent Type. Give this fellow one provocative question and unless you know how to handle the situation, you'll be listening to his answer for the next 30 minutes.

He may wear you out, but I'll take him any day in preference to the Strong, Silent boy. He's hungry for an audience, and in you he has a captive one. He sometimes feels obligated to the point where he almost thinks he has to buy. His wife probably pays no attention to his lengthy speeches. He sees that you're listening, and your respect warms him up. The nicest part of it is that he is usually selling himself all the time he's talking.

You can develop personal opening remarks that will encourage friendly conversation as a preliminary to the sales solicitation. You can follow that up with questions that deal directly with your product or service—the more directly, the better. Remember that the man finally has to say something before you make a sale. He must say "Yes" when you ask for the order, or your labor's lost. The sooner you get him talking, the easier that final "Yes" becomes for him to say.

Later on, you're going to come to Point 17, which deals with getting the customer to ask questions. But before he will ask questions, you must get him to talk. This may sound foolish, but getting him to say anything, no matter how irrelevant, is important. You have to establish communication with the man before you can arrive at the common ground you're aiming for, and you don't have communication without dialogue. When you do all the talking, you don't really establish anything except that you can talk—which you already know, and which, with the proper coin, will get you a cup of coffee in any restaurant. But that won't make a sale for you.

I recall trying to sell a man who had the reputation of being a gregarious guy and a pleasant man with salesmen. I soon began wondering if I had something that even my friends wouldn't tell me about, because I absolutely could not get this fellow to say anything.

I knew that sailing was a hobby of his, so I tried to discuss sailing with him. Nothing happened. I'd been told that he was a hi-fi buff. No response there either. I tried everything I could think of to get this man to say something, and felt more and more like I was in his personal deep-freeze. He just wasn't with it.

It Was Trouble With the Boss

Finally, in desperation, I said, "Mr. Franklin, everybody who knows you, and we have a number of mutual friends, has told me that you're one of the easiest men to talk to that I'll ever find in this business. Up to this point, I have the feeling that you're one of the most difficult. Did I say something to offend you? Did I do something to irritate you? I'd like to know."

He stared at me for a few seconds and then grinned. "Mr. Anderson," he said, "you haven't done anything to offend me. But I'm damned well irritated. And it's no fault of yours. Ten minutes before our appointment, I came from a meeting with the chairman of the board. There may be a jackass of greater stature somewhere in the jackass world, but if you'd like a quick bet, I'll give you odds that you can't find one. He's without question the most unreasonable, irritating man that ever headed a company of this size. I came back to my office frustrated and mad. I'm still frustrated and mad. I know it's completely unfair to you, but I haven't heard much of what you said, because I'm seething."

Another Story That Helped

The dam broke. He told me a long story of how he'd planned to expand his sales force and augment his advertising. He had worked out a complete proposal that explained every detail and justified every part of the plan.

The board chairman had treated him like a little boy and had informed him that he wasn't interested in proposals on how to spend more money. His interest, the board chairman said, was in making more money for the stockholders, and apparently he was the only person in the organization who had that viewpoint.

I told him the story about William Wrigley, Jr., and Jim Offield riding together to California on the Super Chief.

"The company had a fine year," Jim Offield observed, "and showed a nice profit. But you spent five million dollars on advertising. We're the best known chewing gum company in the country. Now, if you had spent two million on advertising instead of five, there'd have been an additional three-million-dollar profit."

"Jim," Mr. Wrigley said, "how fast do you suppose we're traveling right now?"

Looking out the window, Jim answered, "It must be close to 80 miles an hour."

63

"I'd say so, too," Mr. Wrigley nodded. "I wonder why the stupid fools don't get rid of the engine and let us coast in to California."

The man got the point of the story. He grew more and more enthusiastic, telling me how he was going to use it with the chairman of the board. He thanked me for giving him the ammunition he needed—and his whole attitude toward me and my sales solicitation changed completely. I left with a substantial order and a friend it would be a pleasure to see again.

That was an unusual case, but the man who is consistently silent during a sales solicitation isn't at all uncommon. With the product or service you're selling, what can you do to encourage him to open up? Do you have any provocative questions you can ask that will bring him out of his shell? Do your questions stay on the sales line you've mapped out?

There are really only two problems under Point 4—the customer who talks too much and the customer who doesn't talk at all. Yes, there are only two problems, but they can be big ones if you're not prepared to handle them.

On the first few points, you've had some "starter" questions tossed at you. Now, on Point 4, what starter questions can *you* devise to start a mute prospect talking?

5. Did I give the customer a reason for buying from me rather than from another salesman?

The Roughneck, one of the six sales managers who took part in the creation of the 20 Points, disagreed violently with Point 5 at first. This hard-bitten curmudgeon said he didn't *want* his salesmen to make themselves an integral part of every sale. He insisted that he wanted to be able to replace any salesman at any time without danger of losing business.

The other men pointed out to him that he would be far better off if his salesmen were so good that he wouldn't *dare* to replace them.

This cantankerous coot wasn't alone. I've since run across other sales managers who felt the same way.

From *your* standpoint as a salesman, it's a matter of self-preservation and self-advancement to make yourself a part of every sale, regardless of how your sales manager feels. And don't feel badly about it if your sales manager doesn't agree with you. In helping yourself, you're helping him and the company, because you make more good sales.

Your Home Telephone Number

Just as you give a customer a reason to buy a product, you give him a reason to buy from you. You try to make yourself an integral part of each sale. Maybe I can give you a few ideas.

One salesman always gives his customer a business card on which he writes his home telephone number. "If you have any problem after working hours," he explains, "call me at home. If I'm not there, who-ever answers will know where to reach me. And if you call the plant during the day, ask for me so that I can follow through and see that your problem is solved immediately."

I asked this fellow if any customers ever *did* call him at home after working hours. "Oh, sure," he said.

"But doesn't that get annoying?" I asked.

"Nope," he said. "When a customer makes a call like that, he's *my* customer from that time on. I'll put up with a lot more inconvenience than a phone call to get a personal customer. And the calls aren't all complaints, you know," he added.

"What are they, then?" I asked.

"Orders," he grinned. "You'd be surprised how often somebody decides to place an order outside of working hours."

Another salesman, who travels, has a little card. He pays for the printing, himself. His picture is on the card, along with this wording: "You just placed an order with the Blank Name Company, through Kermit Kay, who values your business. Delivery of the merchandise should be on or about .... Should there be any goods damaged in shipment or anything unsatisfactory in any way in the fulfillment of this order, call Mr. Kay collect at MAin 3-2200. Mr. Kay wants to follow through on your order with the best service that is humanly possible."

A Hobby Goes to Work

He clips that card to the customer's copy of the order. The number of complaints is negligible, he says, "but every customer feels that if there *had* been anything wrong, good old Kermit Kay would have taken care of it pronto."

One salesman who is a camera bug says he has made many friends in business with a simple little device. Once the order is signed, he

Did I give the customer a reason for buying from me?

says to the customer, "Say, I just got an idea. This is my first sale to your company. I happen to have my Leica with me, so lets go through the motions of signing the order again and I'll have your secretary snap us. I'll send you a print as soon as it's ready."

He does his own developing and enlarging. When he's made an enlarged print, he puts it into an inexpensive frame, after signing it, "Thanks for a much appreciated order." He says the customers actually write and thank him for the pictures and that they always mention it on subsequent calls.

"What makes the idea a real winner from my standpoint," he says, "is that they don't think of having placed an order with the A-One Company; they think of the picture as a record of the order they placed through *me*."

Don't Be Afraid to Get Involved

There are so many ways you can make yourself a part of the order. When a customer is in a legitimate hurry for merchandise, instead of printing "Rush" on an order blank, you call your office and talk to the right person to get the order expedited.

A salesman friend sells cosmetics to retail stores. And whenever he gets an order from a new customer, he sticks around and shows the salespeople in that store how to do a good selling job. When he sells a new product in the line, and they're frequent, he shows the salespeople in all his customers' stores how to do the best possible demonstration.

One retail salesman made a friend of me when I made a purchase from him. I told him I'd like to have the suit of clothes he'd sold me for the weekend. It needed alterations and would miss the delivery schedule. Without a second's hesitation, he told me that he, himself, would bring it to my home in the evening. I later learned that he lived about 20 miles from my suburban home.

Another salesman of my acquaintance follows through on every order. He writes or calls the dealer four or five times to see if the display worked out all right, how the product is moving, and what, if any, the problem areas are. One of this man's customers told me, "I honestly feel like John is a partner in my business, the interest he takes."

Sometimes you make yourself part of a sale by showing patience, by answering what seem like silly questions without showing irritation. You explain things about your product or service that seem obvious. I've had people tell me, after a sale was closed, "I'd have bought something like this a long time ago, but salesmen didn't seem to want to give me a thorough explanation. Now that you've shown me how everything works, I realize that some of my questions were a little stupid—but I didn't know that when I asked. And you were willing to take the time to satisfy me."

It's sometimes possible to make yourself part of a sale by bringing someone else into the selling picture. My wife was buying some furniture—or trying to buy it—and she wasn't sure what she wanted. She went to several good stores without making a purchase. And then she went to a store where the salesman said, "I don't honestly know, myself, what would be right in the area you describe. Let's talk to the interior decorator." The decorator solved by wife's problems to her complete satisfaction—but it was the salesman who won her gratitude. No other salesman had tried to help her.

Good Examples From Retailing

I overheard a saleswoman in the dress section of a department store talking to a customer. "Now that you've picked this dress," she said, "I want you to see what a difference a plain white linen hanky in the pocket will make." She even showed the woman a trick way to arrange the handkerchief so it would stay in place, and her customer was delighted.

My dad had a jewelry store for many years, and he always waited for Steve King to call on him to do the major part of his buying. I asked him if the company Steve King represented was that much better than other jewelry wholesalers. "No," he told me, "but Steve King is that much better than other salesmen." If Steve thought Dad

Did I give the customer a reason for buying from me?

was ordering too few of a particular item, he pressed gently for a larger order. If he thought Dad was being overoptimistic about another item, he held him down. He talked Dad into putting in a line of inexpensive gift items for card-party prizes and similar things—and told my father where to buy them to get the best prices. He even showed Dad how to set up the department to make it attractive, and helped him write the ad announcing it.

Dad knew quite a bit about making yourself a part of the sale, himself. Whenever he sold a watch, he instructed the buyer to bring it in once a month for three or four months for chronometer adjustment. He put his watch sales in a tickler file—and if the buyer *didn't* come in to have the timepiece adjusted, he got a telephone call reminding him that he should do it.

Making yourself a part of the sale is one of those things that separates the pro from the amateur, the man from the boy.

Separates Pro From Amateur

On the retail floor, there's seldom time enough to use the personal points to their full advantage on volume items. Even here, though, knowledge of these points makes a difference.

When I was running a country weekly newspaper in Nebraska, a hardware salesman, "Bunt" Fleetwood, managed to make himself a part of every sale—and some of the sales were mighty small. But farmers for many miles around came in to fill their hardware needs with Bunt, simply because they enjoyed doing business with him. His pleasantries, his obliging manner, everything about him made him an important part of his sales.

The variety-store notions salesgirl who has a bright, pleasant personality will do twice the business a sullen, morose girl will do.

Some people will argue, citing such an example, that you don't need the 20 Points to sell notions, and I disagree heartily. You need the 20 Points to sell anything. The reason the points are seldom used at such places as notions counters is simply this:

In such places, there's much more buying than selling. In many, many cases, the so-called salesman's job is not to sell at all but simply to help people buy.

It's my further belief that one of the reasons for the success of self-service retail stores is that the caliber of salesmanship on many retail floors is so miserably low. Right now, there are department store items I have to buy—and I put it off as long as I can because I dread the prospect of the salesman I may have to suffer.

If you're an extrovert with a likable personality, you start with an edge over many salespeople. Given the same selling tools as a lack-luster introvert, your personality can be the one big difference. If you happen to be a shy, colorless person, and you want to sell, you must make up your mind to overcome your personality.

If you get nothing from the 20-Point System except an understanding of the personal points—the "you" element in sales—you'll have fundamental knowledge that, properly applied, simply has to make you a better salesman.

Some salesmen will regard these first five points as slightly on the intangible side. They'll want meat-and-potato selling tools.

A Review of the Personal Points

The next seven points are the solid backbone of selling, the Proof Points, where we get down to the hard, practical, reason-why part of selling. But before we go on to them, try to apply the first five points to yourself and what you sell:

1. What are the best ways for you to make a favorable impression on your prospective customers? How should you dress? How should you act? What are your best opening approaches to get a prospect's personal interest?

2. Do you talk from the customer's viewpoint? Do you need to change terminology? Do you need to change *your* viewpoint? How can you keep from being too obviously eager to close? What can you do

Did I give the customer a reason for buying from me?

that you haven't been doing to show your sympathy for the prospect's problems and interests?

3. How can you find the strongest desire or need on the customer's part? How can you capitalize on it? Do you have a sales approach that *will* capitalize on *any* desire or need? List the ones you can satisfy, and decide how best to appeal to them.

4. How do you encourage the customer to do part of the talking right at the outset of your solicitation? How do you get him involved?

5. What are the best ways in which you can make yourself a part of every sale?

And now, on to proof, the world of facts. As a world-champion hog caller once said, "You've got to have more than power in your voice. You've got to convince the hogs that you have something for them."

The Proof Points

Nobody really needs to emphasize the importance of the Proof Points in selling. Perhaps they've been emphasized too much. At least, other elements haven't received nearly enough consideration by comparison.

In selling done by a manufacturer, particularly, proof is stressed almost to the exclusion of everything else. It's not hard to understand, because the manufacturer *has* proof of the quality of his merchandise, and he wants to be sure that his market gets that proof, too. His "sales training" course is, as I've said earlier, quite often nothing but product information.

Product Knowledge Means Work

Now, there's nothing wrong with product information. As a buyer, I've run up against altogether too many salesmen who didn't know nearly enough about what they were selling.

For example, I'm a hi-fi bug, and since I did considerable work for a major manufacturer of hi-fi equipment, I had to learn about the field. The misstatements that hi-fi salesmen make about equipment, its functions, its quality, and its points of difference are appalling. Start pinning these bluffers down and they suddenly lose all interest in selling you anything.

The head of one successful discount house had trouble getting his salespeople to inform themselves about the products they were selling, many of which were major appliances. He finally found a way to solve the problem.

Each new man was given an instruction course on some one item—usually, a vacuum cleaner. He wasn't allowed to show customers any other item until he had proved that he was capable of it.

The plan worked like this. The men were working on a small salary and substantial commission. They wanted to be able to sell everything in the store. But before they could move out of the cleaner section, they had to study the sales manual on another item. Once they had passed a written examination based on that sales manual, they were permitted to sell the item. And in spite of the general lack of interest on retail salesmen's part toward learning product specifications, warranties, etc., it was amazing how quickly these salesmen became well-informed.

Proof Points Are Complex

The Proof Points are the one area in selling where there is absolutely no excuse for doing a bad job. Some people may not have the personality to do a superb job on the personal points. Some may not be good enough as ad-libbers to do a bang-up job on the opposition points. And there are some would-be salesmen who are just plain scared to death to try to close a sale. There are others who instinctively try too soon.

But the Proof Points are solid, tangible things—the facts, the hard realities.

They are used wrongly almost as often as they're used rightly. You can bore the daylights out of a prospective buyer with too much dull proof.

And the Proof Points are almost never the only consideration. Quite often, they are nothing more than the justification for a customer to buy something he's already decided he wants.

For example, a candy bar urges you to buy Jim-Dandy Candy for Vitamin B-1 and Quick-Energy Pickup. Now, I never knew anybody in my life who bought a candy bar for either Vitamin B-1 or quick energy pickup. The advertiser, however, knows that many people feel guilty about spending money for sheer enjoyment. If they have the waistline battle that I do, they feel guilty in that area, too. So the advertiser offers a justification. You may not believe what he says, but it gives you an excuse for enjoying yourself.

To close a sale, you first convince a customer that he should buy, and one of the ways you convince him is with proof. The more convincing the proof, the easier the sale.

The prospect, no matter how friendly, is selfish and cautious. No matter how much he wants what you're selling, he needs cold, hard proof of value. He wants assurance that he's making a sound purchase.

The Proof Points have been called the solid backbone of the sales solicitation. Mail-order catalogues sell primarily on proof, but please don't get the idea that you can do likewise. I've known salesmen who were walking encyclopedias of product information who couldn't sell dollar bills for 50 cents.

Most Companies Furnish Proof

Without product information, however, you have nothing to build on. You can't possibly be convincing, because you don't really know what you're trying to prove.

One of the few things that many salesmen know about selling is the facts about their product or service. Most employers are good about furnishing product information to their men, although in widely variat degrees of interest and usefulness.

Some salesmen who are admirably informed get careless about proof. After they've made a few calls on a prospect, they make the mistake of thinking he already knows as much about the product or service as there is to be known. It's easy to be so close to your work that you think everyone else is familiar with it, too.

You've seen salesmen who hand out product information by the shovelful in such a drab, impersonal manner that they give the impression of being walking spec sheets.

Remember that product information should always prove something to the customer. If it doesn't, it's a waste of time to even mention it.

A Case of Too Many Figures

On my first newspaper advertising job, I was classified ad manager of the Sioux City (Iowa) *Tribune*. Real estate firms were heavy users of classified, and one of the big ones advertised exclusively in the opposition paper. I called on this tough guy with charts and figures enough for a two-hour speech. I harangued this man with proof—proof that he was making a bad mistake by not advertising in the *Tribune*. I finally summed up the proof and asked for the order.

He said the first thing I'd permitted him to say. What he said was, "No."

"But why?" I persisted. "I've given you every reason in the world to become a *Tribune* advertiser. Now, why won't you do it?"

"There's no damn law that says I gotta tell you why I will or won't do anything," he answered. "But I'll give you one reason. After listening for over an hour to those mumbo-jumbo figures of yours, I'm so sleepy I'm gonna take a nap."

I had thrown so much proof at him that all I'd really proved was what a bore I could be.

The hard-sell, one-call salesman nearly always depends more on proof points than on anything else. Hugh Hogan, a really great high-pressure salesman, used proof points to the nth degree. And he pointed out something to me. "I'm meeting this man for the first and last time, so I have to point out everything that might keep him from letting this fleeting opportunity get away from him."

Hugh at work was intense—and believable. I don't believe he ever used a proof point that he couldn't back up. He sold products and services of genuine merit, and one of the great things he had, I think, was an ability to make what he was talking about seem for the moment to be of paramount importance. Every fact he tossed at a potential buyer seemed to be a vital one.

When an insufficiently informed young salesman asked Hugh the secret of his sales as opposed to the youngster's misses, Hugh answered, "It's always nice to know what you're talking about. I do, and you don't. It's that simple."

And before you pass that off as heavy-handed sarcasm, how many salesmen have you contacted recently who impressed you as genuine authorities on what they were selling? I can think of only two who've talked to me within the past four months whose recommendations I would accept without further checking. These two men, and only these two, had the information a buyer has the right to expect of any salesman who calls on him.

I can be tolerant of the salesman who flubs the personal points in selling, as I said. Maybe nobody's even told him that there is a personal element in making sales. Perhaps his sales manager is unaware of the selling uses of personality, too.

The One Intolerable Weakness

And the salesman who gets upset by questions, who doesn't know how to field opposition, is understandable. Sometimes objections are mighty hard to handle, particularly when they're legitimate ones.

The salesman who doesn't know how or when to close has my sympathy. Maybe he's choked up. Maybe nobody has ever told him he should ever ask for an order. Don't raise your eyebrows. I've sat through entire sales training courses where asking for the order was never even mentioned. Apparently, management assumed that if you'd done a good job, the customer would grab you by the lapels and plead for a chance to buy.

But let me repeat, the one thing of which I'm completely intolerant in a salesman is lack of knowledge about what he's selling. It's inexcusable. The least likely salesman has been exposed to product information. He knows, without even being told, that he should have it. If he doesn't have it, I don't even want to talk to him. There are pleasanter ways to waste time.

Yet, you'll find the uninformed salesman at every level of selling. How he manages to survive, I don't know. How a company that will send out such a representative manages to stay in business is even more of a mystery.

Recently I had a salesman trying to sell me an order of carpeting for my home admit that he didn't even know the composition of the fabric in the carpeting. Another salesman didn't know whether an inexpensive suit was wash-and-wear or not. A paint salesman trying to sell me a new kind of house paint finally admitted, when pressed, that he didn't have the faintest idea of whether this paint had been adequately tested or not, or what its points of superiority were supposed to be.

The Proof Points are the one part of a sales solicitation where no excuse can be accepted. To even call yourself a salesman, you must know them. To be a good salesman, you must know how to apply them and how to glamorize them so that they'll really work for you.

6. Did I properly convey the backgrounds and merits of the company I represent?

The good name of your company is one of your most valuable selling tools. If you assume that the potential customer already knows all there is to know about the merits of your firm, you have no right to make such an assumption.

Just as people prefer to buy from people they like, they prefer to buy from firms they respect. Everyone wants to buy with confidence.

A long number of years in business means to a customer that the company must turn out a good product and do a good job of servicing or it couldn't have maintained its solvency. The rapid rise of a company in an industry in the face of long-established competitors means to a customer that the new company must have something extremely good.

A good research department means that a company is trying to improve its products and its service to its customers.

A good financial statement means that a company has responsibility and solidity. A firm's reputation for standing behind what it sells with guarantees or service can be a tremendous factor.

Fresh, youthful enthusiasm impresses customers. So does established, proven leadership in an organization.

A salesman who isn't proud of the organization he represents has no place in the company and does both himself and his employer a disservice by staying with it.

Did I properly convey the merits of my company?

I've never known a salesman who didn't have some complaints against his employer, some justified and some imaginary. But a good salesman keeps complaints within the family. When the good name of his firm is questioned, he becomes a tiger. Unless you sell the merits of the company you represent, you belittle yourself as well as your firm. You say, in effect, "This outfit I represent isn't much, but I guess it's as good as I can do."

Selling the merits of your company makes sales. One sewing machine, for example, has an edge over competition. Is it because of price? There are other lines that are substantially cheaper. Is it because of exclusive features? I doubt it. Other makes have exclusive features, too. It's the good name of the manufacturer that gives the line its edge.

Your pride in your company should be infectious. It should be proof to the customer that he's not making any mistake when he spends his money with you.

What does your company have to be proud of—things that you can use to help you sell? It must have a number of such things or it wouldn't be in business. And the things it can be proud of must mean benefits to customers.

Make a List of the Good Things

Everybody wants to be successful, so when you prove to the customer that he's dealing with a successful company, you're taking an important step toward making a sale.

Make a list of the things that make the firm you represent a good firm. Don't list anything that isn't true, because you won't do a convincing job of presenting untruths. After you've completed your list, think of how best to talk about those things to prospective customers. Try to determine which points would most impress the people you're selling.

Once you've determined what to say about your organization, you're ready. And when you've completed a sales solicitation and ask yourself, "Did I properly convey the background and merits of the company I represent?," and can answer with an emphatic, enthusiastic "Yes," you've helped yourself, your company, and your customer.

Let me make another point, though, before we go on. Sometimes it isn't the salesman's fault that he fails to present his company in a good light. If the company furnishes you with cheap, shabby sample cases, what you say isn't going to make up for the deficiency. If your business cards are poorly printed on cheap paper, it's bound to make a poor company impression.

There are other ways the company can damage its image—and it should be doing its part to help you make the right company impression. If it isn't doing the job, talk to your sales manager about the problem. Even if he doesn't do anything about it, you're on record.

One salesman I know watches the stock market. If the price on stock in his company is up, he invariably says to a customer, "Say, did you read today's stock market report?" Then he mentions where the stock stands, with the comment, "Our company sure must be doing a lot of things right."

Another carries large-sized glossy prints of his firm's new plant, which happens to be beautiful. He mentions, incidentally, that growth made the new plant possible, and throws in a few words of why that growth has taken place.

Uses Design Prizes As Booster

One salesman carries a list with him of the several design prizes his company has won. "I think product design is one reason why our organization has become the greatest in its field. Good design helps not only the company but the retailer and the consumer," he says. "It's nice to represent a company that's always a leader in design."

A salesman who got a flattering letter of commendation from the president of his company carries that letter with him and shows it to his customers. "I work for the greatest bunch of guys in the world," he says. "They don't forget to let you know when they think you're doing a good job. And they know, because they keep their eyes open. They

Did I properly convey the merits of my company?

know when a customer does a good job, too, and they try to reward him for it. There's a personal quality about our company that you have to like."

I commented to this fellow that it certainly was nice of the president to write that letter.

"Well," he grinned, "of course, I *asked* him to write it. My chief competition is big and impersonal. I thought it'd be a good approach to sell the personal attention our company gives."

Another salesman never fails to tell a new prospect about the insurance and pension benefits his company gives, and stresses that they're the best in the business. "These people have loyalty and integrity," he says. "They show it to employees as well as customers. I'm proud to be working for them."

Annual Report Is Another Tool

A salesman of my acquaintance works for a really progressive company whose annual stockholders' report is a humanized masterpiece, loaded with four-color pictures and explanations written so that a minor stockholder can understand them. This salesman asked for and got enough copies of the report to leave one with every customer or prospect he called on. His sales manager told me, "Eddie's customers must have been impressed, because 14 of them bought stock in the company after they'd seen the annual report." The regrettable thing to me is that none of the other salesmen in the company thought of doing what Eddie did.

Some years ago, the 3M Company was the subject of a fascinating book, *The Brand of the Tartan*. One 3M salesman got a number of copies of the book, and ran what amounted to a lending library with his customers, until his copies were worn out. He thought that the people who read the book would be impressed and that sales would be easier for him. All 3M salesmen tell their customers about Minnesota Mining research, and the story is one that always leaves a prospect feeling he'd do well to become associated with such a great organization.

A salesman for a fine ethical drug company carries the series of institutional ads his employer runs, and shows them with great pride to every customer or prospect. He says, "If you didn't know anything about the company and saw these ads for the first time, you'd know that we must be leaders, wouldn't you?"

When the head of a factory that's located in a small community won the town's Outstanding Citizen award, the company's top salesman put the newspaper story onto a copying machine and sent copies to every customer and prospect in his territory. The story told much about the company as well as its head. Then when this salesman called on his customers, he asked them if they'd read the story he sent them. If they hadn't, he just happened to have another copy with him.

Showing pride in your company does more than help you to make a sale. Being associated with such a fine firm and being so enthusiastic about it increases your stature with the customer. To put it simply, the customer reasons that the better a company is, the better its representatives must be.

Point 6 is one of the easiest to do a good job on, because most employers can give a salesman all the proof of their merits that he can use. But what are the outstanding merits of the firm you represent that will be most impressive to your customers? Remember, you should be talking from the customer's viewpoint, not your own, and what sold you on the company may be of little interest to the man who's buying from you. To arrive at a good answer, you might start by asking yourself, "What factors are most responsible for my company's success?" Put them all down, and then eliminate the ones that apply to employees but not to customers.

If you were representing a brand new company in an old field, how would you handle Point 6?

If your company depends on low prices to get business, what would your approach to Point 6 be? If it produces quality merchandise at high prices?

If a story had just appeared that your company was in trouble with the Food and Drug Administration, what would you say?

7. Was I able to tell the customer at least one new, beneficial thing about the product or service I'm selling?

You've undoubtedly noticed how often the word "New" is used in advertising—overused, sometimes—and sometimes, too, used without justification. But "New" or "Improved" is an appeal with great interest value, the same kind of interest value that gets readers for newspapers. You need that news value in your sales solicitation.

No matter how good a phonograph record is, you get tired of it when you've heard it 50 times. When you stop to think about it, there's not really much reason for a customer to listen to you unless you have something new to tell him, is there?

Something new? I should say, something new to *him*. It may be old stuff to you, but if it's new to him, you'll get his attention, interest, and respect.

Sometimes you have to dig to find news value in your product or service, but it's always there.

What About Your Advertising?

Your company's advertising plans may be important news to the customer. Those plans may mean more profit for him, or faster, easier sales.

I remember doing a so-called "loading" job for a candy manufacturer who was going into television for the first time in the company's history.

20-Point System for Guaranteed Sales Success

At a meeting of candy jobbers, we showed the half-hour film of the first show, complete with the company's commercials. We had figures on the audience the show would get every week, all over the United States. We told the jobbers why this particular show had been chosen, why it was slanted the way it was, and why the commercials were being done by the star of the show.

We took enough orders at that meeting so that the show had at least paid a substantial part of its cost before it ever went on the air.

Now, there was nothing new or different about the product. The news was a new, aggressive, mass advertising program. Believe me, news of this kind is always welcomed, because the distributor knows that an extra advertising push will almost inevitably create more retail demand—and he doesn't want to be caught short.

Few Chain Saws on Broadway

A few years ago, a chain saw manufacturer had been spending quite a chunk of its advertising money on network radio. I pointed out to management that a good part of what they were buying was big-city circulation. And the number of people in New York, Chicago, Los Angeles and other large cities who buy chain saws isn't going to do much for anybody.

So we developed a new radio approach. Instead of one-minute spots in a network news show, we created our own five-minute show, starring Pat Buttram. The shows were recorded, and we put them on stations right in the communities—mostly small ones—where there was a good chain saw market.

The annual meeting of the manufacturer's distributors was held in Kansas City. We secretly bought five minutes of time on a Kansas City radio station and flew Buttram in from the West Coast. A few minutes before the show was due to go on the air, every distributor was given a little transistor radio tuned to the Kansas City station, and told to turn the set on.

A part of the new idea was to have what's called a "local cut-in" at the conclusion of each show, with a local announcer coming on

Was I able to tell the customer at least one new benefit?

and saying, "For a demonstration of this saw, go to the Blank Hardware Store at 999 Oak Street."

The applause was thunderous at the conclusion of the show—and then, to put the icing on the news cake, Pat Buttram sauntered onto the stage and asked, "Well, fellas, how do you like it?"

Did the news sell the distributors? Well, the company had set a goal of taking orders for 10,000 saws at this convention. Instead, they took orders for close to 50,000.

I recall two Motorola sales convention shows I wrote, in which Bob Galvin wanted to break important news.

At the first convention, the important news was the first table-model TV set to sell for under $150. We had a real fire engine, complete with firemen, come clanging down the wide center aisle. As two firemen rushed onto the stage, concealing a package between them, somebody hollered. "Where's the fire?" And the sales manager answered dramatically, whipping the cover off the TV set, "Fire, hell! It's the first television set to retail at under $150—the hottest thing that's ever hit the industry."

"The Big Look" Was an Elephant

At the other convention, the news was the biggest yet. And we broke that piece of news by delivering the set to the stage on an elephant that paraded down the center aisle with lettering on both its sides which said, "The Big Look."

Even a minor change in design can be important news. If it weren't important, the company wouldn't have gone to the expense of making it. I've seen good salesmen get extra-large orders on nothing more than a change in packaging. If you don't think a change in package design can be important, find out what it has done on many occasions to create major sales increases.

But let's suppose that you're selling a package-goods item and that your competitors have changed their package design. They've come up with what seems to you to be a mighty attractive job. But your company has decided after much deliberation *not* to change its package. Hardly news. Scarcely beneficial news, certainly.

But wait! Why did your firm decide to keep the old package? The management spent several thousand dollars on package research and got some extremely interesting information.

In store shelf tests, 80% of the customers reached for your old package in preference to your competitor's new one. A motivational research study showed that your old package represented dependability to 69% of the women interviewed. Every test showed that package changes were being made by competition to try to compete with your old package. It was consistently maintaining its leadership —still the champion—and still the easiest to stack for shelf and counter displays.

This news could be the basis for a special store display by your retail customers. And the preference for your product shown by the survey could bring a review of comparative space and size of orders on the two products.

A new application or use of a product or service, tried by another customer, is interesting news—beneficial news.

Changes in discount structure can be news—worthy and beneficial. So can changes in customer policy.

Remember, It May Be New to Him

Successful business organizations make news all the time, sometimes without realizing it. But let's assume that nothing new is happening in your field right now. How do you tell the customer at least one beneficial, new thing? Well, you may have to slant an old benefit so that it's new to him. There is always a new *slant* on some proof point, and the new approach gives news value to your sales solicitation. It also keeps you from being a walking version of a mailing piece.

If you only call on your customers once a year, it's easy to come up with news value—but you should try to be thinking of new, bene-

Was I able to tell the customer at least one new benefit?

ficial things constantly. The more exciting and beneficial news you get into your sales story, the more sales you'll make. And thinking about news value will keep you out of a rut. It'll keep you on your toes mentally. Regard it as a challenge to your ingenuity.

His News—"No New Model This Year"

One of the greatest "news" selling jobs I ever encountered came from the factory representative of one of the smaller appliance manufacturers. Sales had been so far below anticipation that the company couldn't afford to come out with its usual annual new models. This fellow covered distributors with, "Have you heard the news? We're so well pleased with the current models that we're going to stick with them for another year. No model changes of any kind. Our management recognizes a good thing when they see it, and they're smart enough to capitalize on it. This can be a great selling point for you. Housewives don't like to have obsolete models of appliances, and you can sell the fact that *your* line doesn't become obsolete. It also means that if you have any of this year's models in stock at the end of the season, you won't have to discount them. No matter how good sales are, you know as well as I do that such a thing can happen—but our company is now protecting you on that score. You'll also get the cumulative effect of our advertising, because we won't have to begin all over again on a new model and a whole new selling job. Your men won't have to be trained in a new approach or learn about different features to emphasize. You've got a strong selling point, too, when you tell customers that you represent the only company in the field that didn't have to bring out a new model. I was so pleased about the news that I wanted to get right out and tell you about it before you heard it somewhere else."

That "news approach," I must add, wasn't wholly successful, but this fellow did a better job of holding distributors than any other man in the company—and with the savings the company made the following year, it was able to survive what might have been a disaster. Making good news out of adversity as this factory rep did should deserve some kind of a medal. And the following year, when the company was able to compete with new models, he went back again with great news. "I have the best news you've heard in a long time," he said. "Thanks to the savings we made last year by not changing models, we're able to come out this year with the most revolutionary, beautiful, salable new models you've ever had an opportunity to sell."

Toastmaster, with a widely accepted line of electric toasters, came out with an entirely new toaster design a few years ago. It was the first really pronounced change in toaster design in many years. And did the Toastmaster sales force ever make news of it! Every Toastmaster dealer was sold right to the hilt that the new design was the greatest thing that had happened to toast since sliced bread. Toastmaster management felt from its research that the new design would be more convenient and more attractive—but they didn't want to sell too hard on those things until the toasters were actually on the market. Rightly, I think, they stressed the news value of the design change first—and then later sold the benefits of the change, once they'd been reasonably proven. Regardless of how much research they had on what acceptance of the new models would be, they knew that this was an area where dealers would want to see for themselves. Sales potential couldn't be completely proven in advance, but news value could be. It was right there.

Sale Has New Name Each Year

One substantial producer in the soap field has the same special discounts during certain periods every year. But every year, this company's salesmen make exciting news of the upcoming discount. And to make it continue to be newsworthy year after year, they always give the special discount a new name and a new twist. Because it represents a benefit—more profit—buyers accept it as good news regardless of what name it has.

The sales manager of a typewriter company told me that when his organization first took to color in its portables—some of the colors were pretty wild—the news impact alone gave them the biggest in-

Was I able to tell the customer at least one new benefit?

crease in business they'd ever had—and did it before the advertising was even released. "Salesmen bearing the good news did the trick," he said. "And later, when the public got the same news through advertising, dealers unloaded fast."

"Firsts" are always easy to sell if they have any merit. But good "firsts" don't come along every day for any manufacturer or any salesman. Much of the time, you have to dig for news angles.

I guarantee that if you give a few minutes' time and serious thought to the problem every day, you'll come up with better and better approaches. It's like putting. The more you practice, the better you do.

But don't make the mistake, a common one, of telling something about your product merely as news. Always point out the beneficial application of your news to the customer. Make it not only get attention, but help to sell.

When you ask yourself, "Was I able to tell the customer at least one new, beneficial thing about my product or service that he didn't already know?" you're asking, in effect, "Was this sales solicitation any better or any different than those that have failed previously?"

A salesman who shows enthusiasm does better than one who doesn't—and having something newsworthy to talk about generates enthusiasm for you.

What represents the greatest news value inherent in the product or service you're selling? Is there any news value outside the product or service, as in new marketing strategy or a new merchandising plan?

Think of an example of a publicity release your company could issue that would give you news value.

Forgetting facts, what would be the best news if it were true that you could possibly give your customers? How close could you come to that story and stick with the truth?

Assume that you're selling a product that hasn't had a design change in five years. Your three major competitors all had changes last year. What is your news for the customer?

8. Was the customer thoroughly acquainted with *all* the advantages of my product or service by the time I concluded?

We are now on dangerous ground. This point doesn't mean that you conduct a five-or six-hour sales pitch. You don't make yourself a bore by belaboring points the customer already knows.

But you must realize that usually just about all the customer does know is what he learns from you or from your literature and advertising. And while all men like to learn, few men like to study. The customer would *always* rather be told benefits than dig out the information for himself. And the only way you can be sure he knows the features of your line and what they mean to him is to tell him.

Remember back in the personal points where you got the customer to talk while you listened? Well, by getting him to talk, you should have found the areas where he wasn't familiar enough with what you're selling. So now you fill him in. You have no right to assume that he's familiar with anything without checking.

Mail Ads Loaded With Product Information

To do this job concisely and completely, try to write a mail-order ad for whatever you're selling—but try to write it the way a good copywriter writes mail-order copy. Look over some good mail-order ads and analyze them. You'll find that many of them are rather small ads—but they're loaded with product information. They try to sell *all* the advantages, quickly and concisely.

90

Was the customer thoroughly acquainted with *all* the advantages?

When you start working out your own list, I'll almost guarantee that you'll come up with at least one advantage you never used before.

Some reasonably successful salesmen actually have nothing in their favor except a thorough knowledge of Point 8 and how to use it. They don't know much about selling, but they use what they do know to the utmost advantage.

As you've seen, there can be pitfalls in Point 8. And one of the worst pitfalls is in the matter of believability.

The advantages must not only exist but must be believable. Always keep that in mind. When you try to sell a customer on advantages that tax his credulity, you mess up a possible sale.

Benefits Don't Get "Equal Time"

The Wm. Wrigley, Jr., Company has researched every possible benefit to be derived from chewing gum. They have more than enough proof of every benefit to make each one stand up under the most critical examination. But the Wrigley Company doesn't use all the chewing gum benefits in its advertising and selling. Why not? Because they think that some of them, while perfectly true, aren't quite believable to the consumer. They say, in effect, "To attribute miraculous benefits to a little, modestly priced product like chewing gum sounds like we're going too far in product claims."

Your product or service may have some advantages that are entirely true but can't be sold without going into lengthy clinical studies. And far be it from me to argue with the Wrigley Company philosophy. If any benefit's believability is doubtful, forget it. You have enough to talk about without throwing a note of skepticism into your presentation.

Another problem in Point 8 is what, for want of a better term, I'll call "proper weight." You present all the advantages, but you don't give them "equal time" or treat them as being of equal importance. To do so almost invariably confuses the customer.

To start with you'll have to *know* all the advantages of your product or service. And that sometimes takes a bit of doing. I've been in sales seminars where the men got down to work on this point, and as they got rolling, they came up with advantages that their own sales manager had never realized existed.

We listed these advantages in random order at first, as the men thought of them, with no attempt at simplification.

Then, when nobody, including the sales manager, could think of any more advantages, we tried to list them in order of their importance. This step invariably brought elaboration and clarification of some advantages, along with considerable argument. Finally, sometimes quite arbitrarily, we came up with a list.

And then the work really started—the work of simplification. It's always easier to write a long explanation than a short one.

But I'll tell you this. By the time those salesmen had finished simplifying the advantages of their product, the company's advertising department could have taken lessons from them. They wound up with about ten sentences that told a powerful selling story.

A prospect wants to be informed, whether he buys or not. He wants to have learned something in return for the time he's given you. The lack of help some salespeople give potential customers is almost shocking. They seem to feel that if they show the goods and tell the price, they've done their job.

Repetition Works in Oral Selling

It's quite true that you'll sometimes make a mistake when you fill a prospect in on a point you think he doesn't know—but that's a whale of a lot better mistake to make than to overlook the point that might make the sale.

The success of repetition in printed advertising can also work in oral selling—up to a point. If you're going to give the best sales story you possibly can, your customer must end up knowing every beneficial thing you can tell him.

Was the customer thoroughly acquainted with *all* the advantages?

What do we mean by that word "advantages"?

We use it almost interchangeably with the word, "benefits." Certain features may offer an advantage that translates into convenience. Lightweight aluminum construction may be an advantage that translates into economy. A special door lock may translate into safety. A special motor may translate into performance or economy. A baked enamel finish or anything beautiful about your product may translate into personal importance.

Note that Point 8 does *not* say, "all the features." It says "all the advantages."

You Sell Benefit by Benefit

You sell advantages, one by one. If you find that a customer's major interest is economy, you slant every feature you can to the economy angle. You even make the service warranty an appealing benefit.

Many sales training programs actually deal with nothing but Point 8. They tell you to sell the glamour, not the gizmo.

Some sales training programs instruct the salesman to sell feature by feature—and the people who helped me prepare the 20-Point System disagree with this. We say that you sell benefit by benefit.

For example, you sell the economy benefit of an automatic washing machine. You show that it uses less water, thanks to a special filtering system on rinses. Then you show that its unique, patented agitator makes it possible to use about half the laundry soap you would use in an ordinary washer. You show what a saving that can be to the specific customer. You point out that the size of the tub enables one to do a family wash with at least one less load. The special temperature control designed to give water the right temperature for every kind of fabric means reduction of loss by shrinkage.

If the customer has expressed a primary interest in economy, you really dwell on that particular advantage and prove that certain features such as those just mentioned add up to the most economical washer on the market.

Then you go ahead, and sell the advantage of convenience, showing how the automatic controls take the last gram of drudgery out of washday. The special lid that makes removal of the laundry from the tub simpler than it has ever been before is another convenience. The instructions for water temperature for all fabrics, including the new synthetics, right on the dial of the water temperature control save the trouble of looking in a manual every time you want to wash a delicate fabric. You point out every advantage of convenience to be found in the machine.

Then perhaps, you go on to durability, selling the stainless steel tub that is durable far beyond any tub ever before put into a washer. You talk about the baked enamel finish that simply will not rust off.

You sell advantage by advantage, or benefit by benefit, whichever term you prefer. If you deviate from this practice and try to sell feature by feature, you'll find yourself getting into the most confused and confusing hodgepodge of miscellaneous information to be imagined. It will not only confuse the customer but is guaranteed to confuse you, the salesman.

Many Ways to Demonstrate

You make the customer acquainted with the advantages in a number of ways, the most obvious of which is pointing out the feature that gives the product the advantage. Other ways which are covered in other points are by demonstration, the experience of other people (the testimonial), and by use of the sales materials your company furnishes.

On the advantage that is most important to the customer, you may make the customer acquainted with it in all the ways mentioned.

A retail salesman selling color TV sets tells me that most of the people he sells claim they are shopping for price. This man happens to be selling one of the more expensive lines.

So he says, "I think what you mean is value, isn't it? A set that has really bad color should have an extremely low price—but it

Was the customer thoroughly acquainted with *all* the advantages?

wouldn't be much of a value. There are sets *priced* lower than the one you seem to be interested in—but there's no other set I know of that offers comparable value.

"For example, our picture tube has a three-year warranty. Most picture tubes carry a one-year warranty. Let's say that picture-tube insurance would cost you $35 a year. You're getting $70 worth of extra value right there. A comprehensive service policy sells for roughly $80 a year. We've kept a record of service calls on this particular set—on every unit we've sold. And do you know what the average service cost per year is? Ten dollars. Joe Doe who lives in your part of town has one of these sets that's 5 years old—and his total service cost has been $30.

Price—or Value?

"Look at this factory guarantee on parts. It's the strongest, most straightforward one you can find. When you look at the catch stipulations in some factory guarantees, you get the idea that the manufacturers of those sets aren't too sure of how much value they're offering.

"This set has a hardwood cabinet that qualifies as good furniture. Cabinets on some of the low-priced sets are metal, painted to look like wood. Others are veneers.

"The sad thing is that the people who buy those inferior sets think about price instead of value, and the initial cost of *any* color television set is too much to risk getting bad value."

This salesman told me about one man who insisted that price was his major consideration. "I happened to know," the salesman said, "that this man's sports car was his pride and joy. So I asked him, 'Do you mean price or value? What I'm getting at is that a Blank compact (he named an extremely cheap one) is priced substantially below a Jaguar. (That was the prospect's car.) But which would you say is the better value?' And the prospect almost sneered, 'The Jaguar—no question about it.' "

Many people hesitate to admit that personal importance or prestige is the Number One benefit they're after. When you find from their reactions to your statements and from remarks they make that PI is what they want most, you sell that benefit tactfully, without saying or intimating that such a benefit means anything to them.

In what order should the advantages be? There is no set order. Most good salesmen try to lead from strength, starting on the advantage they think the prospect wants most. However, an often-used technique is to start with minor features that give this particular benefit and lead up to the features that do the most for it. In short, you build each benefit to a climax.

Really, the order of benefits isn't too important, if you're sure you will cover them all to the satisfaction of the prospect. Many times, dealing with a customer who seemed wary of being oversold, I have started with minor benefits, doing them rather casually. With this approach, the one benefit you've decided is most important becomes the solid climax to your proof, and you can present it more forcefully than you could have if you'd started with it.

To any salesman, weak or strong, who has much experience at selling, it seems to me that Point 8 is the easiest in the whole system to work out logically. You simply start with product or service features, analyze what benefits each offers and why, and then reassemble the information under benefit or advantage classifications.

Organization Is the Key

The place where most salesmen fall down is on good organization of features under benefit headings. And if you aren't properly organized on Point 8, opposition on any feature or benefit can throw you completely off.

Years ago, I was offering a package radio show for sale. It became apparent in the first five minutes of conversation that the show was completely wrong for the prospect. I thought immediately of another

Was the customer thoroughly acquainted with *all* the advantages?

show package we had in our production office that seemed to be just right. So I switched my whole approach to that second show.

And I did fine until I came to the benefits. The man questioned the prestige advantages, which he had said he wanted. I was so disorganized that I couldn't even assemble offsetting prestige benefits in my own mind, let alone be articulate about them. I finally gave up on prestige and went to economy. Here, again—well, no need to be kind —I just plain didn't know what I was talking about. The show would have been ideal. And I not only failed to make the sale, but left this important executive's office knowing that he simply had to think I was a sloppy, completely disorganized salesman. It was an attitude I couldn't have argued against.

A Self-Quiz About Point 8

Today, I wouldn't even call on a man without having Point 8 thoroughly worked out. Let's hope you don't have to learn that lesson in as painful a manner as I did.

Here are a few starter questions to acquaint you with the way to apply Point 8 to anything you may be selling.

1. If you're selling a fine piano, what benefits would you stress that you wouldn't talk about in selling a cheap piano?

2. How many advantages or benefits can you find in the product or service you're selling? What features constitute the proof for each benefit?

3. Read a cigarette ad and then try to analyze the benefits it tried to sell you. What features gave proof of benefit?

4. What approach would you take with a customer who says, "I know all about your product."?

5. Get a spec sheet on a mechanical product, that simply lists features. How many benefits can you find, and what feature classifies under each benefit?

9. Did I induce the customer to participate in the demonstration?

When you buy an automobile, the demonstration ride is the classic sales tool. The salesman tries to get you behind the wheel of the car, because he knows that it always helps him to make a sale.

If the car salesman is following his company's training program, he probably has every minute of that demonstration trip carefully planned. He gets you to prove for yourself what the car will do. He gets you to drive over a rough street to prove riding quality. He gets you to go up a steep incline to prove acceleration. And while you're proving these things to yourself, you are also beginning to acquire a feeling of ownership.

Perhaps the technique isn't as complicated for what you're selling, but the basis is the same.

Leave an Error to Be Found

An old master once taught me a trick in the sale of newspaper advertising space. When he took an ad layout out to show to a customer, he always had a simple but glaring error in it.

The customer nearly always took out a pen or pencil and corrected that error. And the instant he made the change in copy, he began to acquire ownership of that ad.

The Apeco copying machine is sold almost entirely by demonstration. A young salesman came into our office, equipped with one of the

Did I induce the customer to participate in the demonstration?

machines on a caster-carrier. He had scarcely started the demonstration when he had the chairman of our board putting solid objects onto the bed of the machine to be photocopied. He had the president of our company pressing the button to get copies of a magazine article that was still bound into the magazine. At every step of the demonstration, he had somebody in our company participating—and a good deal of the time, the participants were the secretaries who would be using the device if it were purchased.

Before the demonstration was completed, we had a sense of ownership of that machine. The salesman, sensing this, asked for questions, got us to agree with his answers, and asked for the order—which he obtained.

"First I Entertain 'Em, Then I Sell 'Em"

Do you remember the old-time pitchman at the county fair? He was a real artist—and it didn't make much difference what he was selling. He could demonstrate a potato peeler or an automobile spark intensifier with equal facility.

The good pitchman used most of the 20 Points. One of them told me once, "First I entertain 'em to make 'em like me. Then I sell 'em." The demonstration was the backbone of the pitchman's presentation. Now, I can't remember ever having peeled a potato in my life, but I could watch the potato-peeler demonstration all afternoon with fascination. It was entertaining, it was spectacular, it was completely convincing, and, man, did it sell potato peelers!

The pitchman always had people in his "tip" or audience helping him in the demonstration. They could use the product just as well as he could.

I once bought an electric etching gadget from a pitchman. To be objective, an electric etching tool is something I could do without for the rest of my life—but at the time, it seemed only logical to buy one. While I'm not mechanically inclined, to put it mildly, the chap in the audience who tried to use it didn't appear to be the craftsman type, either, and he did some beautiful etching. After I had destroyed a few things I tried to etch, my wife suggested that perhaps the man from the audience had been a "shill." Well, maybe—but anyway, the sales pitch was worth what the etching tool cost me.

When Frigidaire first came out with a Duco finish on the exterior, there was a wonderful sales-floor demonstration. A housewife, looking at a new Frigidaire, would be asked to daub some shoe polish or ink onto it. The salesman would then rub a handful of sand over it. Then he would pour some iodine on and ignite it with a match. After the flame had expired, the woman would be handed a rag and told to wipe off the surface. Miracle of miracles, the finish was unblemished, unspotted, unscratched—and she had cleaned it, herself.

It simply had to be effective selling, to let a housewife prove to herself that she could clean the exterior with so little effort, after it had undergone a spotting far worse than it would receive in her home.

There was a time when I was faced with the problem of stimulating sales on portable dishwashers—and it was a problem. The automatic dishwashers were terrific, but nobody was having much luck selling them.

The manufacturer of this particular dishwasher said, "We don't know the answer. Ask any woman who has one of these portables what she thinks of it and she'll answer, 'I'd rather part with any other appliance in the house. It's the greatest thing I ever had.' But ask any woman who *doesn't* have one and she'll say, just as emphatically, 'I wouldn't have one if you gave it to me.' "

Salesmen Didn't Follow Through

The answer seemed clear to me—demonstration. We prepared a hard-sell television "pitch" film that ran five minutes. You could buy a five-minute commercial spot in those days, but don't try to do it today. What we sold in the film wasn't the dishwasher, itself, but the idea of accepting a free 24-hour trial of the appliance in your own home at no cost. To strengthen the pull, we offered a free set of breakfast dishes to every woman who accepted the trial offer.

Did I induce the customer to participate in the demonstration?

We picked a Southern metropolis for a test campaign. I thought I stirred the salesmen into a frenzy of enthusiasm—and the campaign flopped. We didn't sell quite enough dishwashers to pay for the television time.

And then I found out what had happened. I had aroused the salesmen to a frenzy of lethargy, not enthusiasm. They didn't go at all for the idea of totin' one of those li'l ol' dishwashers out to the lady's home and then maybe havin' to go back the next day and pick it up. So they tried to talk every prospect *out* of the home trial and sell her one of the machines without it. In the few instances where they couldn't convince the woman that she didn't really want them upsettin' things with that li'l machine, sales were good.

Left It a Few Days

The one thing that would have made sales was the one thing the salesmen tried their utmost to avoid.

An International Harvester executive later told me how he had paid his way through college—selling electric refrigerators to farmers.

"I got a beat-up little pickup truck," he said. "Every time I got the time, I put two or three refrigerators on it and went out into the country. Rural electrification had arrived, but for some reason, few farmers had bought electric refrigerators. I'd stop at a farm house and tell the farmer and his wife that the appliance store I represented was trying to assemble information on the farm market for electric refrigerators. I'd like to just plug in one of these babies and leave it for a few days. Then when I come back and get it, you can tell me what you think about it.

"Some of them were suspicious, but I assured them that they didn't have to pay a cent and didn't have to sign anything. It would be pretty hard for me to flimflam you when you have the refrigerator and I don't have anything of yours.

"I'd usually leave the refrigerator three or four days, depending on my schedule, and then I'd go back to pick it up. My greeting was almost identical at every stop, 'What will it cost us for you to leave it here permanently?' It was the easiest selling I ever did in my life."

And he had a little side-note that I can't resist adding, even though it deals with being a good listener rather than with demonstration.

"The darndest thing," he said, "was that the people all took what I said about wanting their reactions seriously. So I made notes on everything they had to say about the refrigerator. I typed up those notes after I graduated and sent 'em in to the manufacturer. And doggoned if I didn't get a check for $700. Nobody in the company had done much thinking about the farm market. They got interested in my notes and checked my sales. I was about the only salesman in the country who was selling electric refrigerators to farmers, and I was hitting about 75%.

It's not too surprising that this man had become an important executive in International Harvester, is it?

When I told him about my dishwasher experience, he laughed. "I could have saved you time, money, and effort," he said. "When I first got into the retail business, I tried to get salesmen to take products out and demonstrate them on the prospect's home grounds—but they couldn't be bothered. They thought they had an easier way of closing sales."

If They Handle, They Usually Buy

I once dealt with a smart little fellow who parlayed a fruit and vegetable stand into a supermarket organization. Instead of having signs around, "Don't pinch the tomatoes," he encouraged customers to pick up the produce. He observed that if they handled it, they usually bought it.

Some products and services are more demonstrable than others. When I had a group of salesmen out covering the country selling a newspaper advertising service, they felt that they were selling an intangible—and they were partly right. But I taught them how to do one extra-good layout using art and copy from the service. They

Did I induce the customer to participate in the demonstration?

would prepare that ad for one of the prospective service buyer's retail merchants and would get one of the advertising salesmen to take the ad out and try to sell it. And when that advertising salesman sold an ad to one of his merchants, an ad prepared from the service, we had a sale.

Even if it isn't practical to carry your product or service with you, it's always possible to get the customer to participate in some way.

A friend of mine, a life underwriter who belongs to the Million Dollar Round Table, got from his insurance company a routine in which the agent fills out information on a man's income and needs and then submits a solicitation based on those figures.

Got Prospect to Fill In Figures

It was a clever, well-thought-through approach, and it got results. But this friend improved on it. Instead of writing down the information himself, he got the prospective customer to fill in the figures. His results were so startingly good that the company sent out a man to determine why the sales tool worked better for him than it did for others.

Remember that, as a salesman, you and the potential customer started out with almost diametrically opposite viewpoints. When you reach the point where you can get the prospect to cooperate with you in the sales solicitation, you're getting close to the point where you can close the sale. The two widely variant viewpoints are beginning to merge.

A woman who shops in a supermarket where she can pick up the merchandise and handle it always buys more than she would if she were placing a telephone order for groceries.

A potential customer who does nothing more than turn a page for you on an easel presentation is helping to sell himself.

My dad once won a contest for selling fountain pens. He did it with an amazing demonstration in which he got the customer to throw the uncapped pen at a soft-pine dart board hard enough to make the point stick in the wood. Then he pulled the pen from the board and had the customer write with it. Practically every time, he sold a fountain pen.

The more impressive your demonstration is, the more it helps to close sales. The more you get a customer to participate in your solicitation, the easier you make it for him to buy.

If you already have a demonstration, is it as effective as it can possibly be? Could anything be done to dramatize it more?

If you don't have a demonstration, how can you have one? We sometimes overlook the obvious. Every time a man tries on a new suit or a woman tries on a hat, they're participating in a demonstration. Setting up a display is a demonstration of how your company helps the retailer to sell merchandise.

A seam rip-test on work clothes can be a powerful demonstration. Walking across the carpet in a new pair of shoes you've just tried on is a demonstration.

When you get a customer to eat a sample of a food product, he's participating in a demonstration. If the product is good, it's a highly effective one.

If you can't think of a good demonstration, which I seriously doubt, you must get the customer to at least participate in your solicitation in some way. He has to participate if you make a sale. Well, he has to sign the order blank, doesn't he?

Simple Demonstrations Are Best

Try to think of a way to demonstrate how a feature of your product or service becomes a benefit—without actually using the product or service. For example, you could demonstrate antistatic effect with two strips of newsprint rubbed briskly enough to load them with static electricity. Hold the two strips together at one end, and the opposite ends will repel each other—until the customer puts his hand between them, at which time they'll jump together.

Did I induce the customer to participate in the demonstration?

Try to think of a demonstration on your product or service that is so simple you can do it almost anywhere, any time. One of the most effective demonstrations I ever saw was on Wynn radiator stop-leak fluid. The service station attendant had a small tin can with half a dozen holes punched into the bottom. He would pour water into the can, which leaked like a sieve. Then he would add a few drops of the stop-leak fluid to the water and the leaking would stop almost instantly.

Today, some sales managers regard demonstration as "old hat." Well, it may be old, but as long as it produces the results it does, it shouldn't be retired.

10. Did I offer the customer at least one advantage he could not obtain from any other source?

Point 10 is one of the greatest sales weapons. I once made an $800,000 sale with it and little else. I recall two instances where friends were worried about making a particular sale that was vital to them. I told them about this point and how I thought they could apply it. I received a handsome gift from them within a week, because they attributed their sale to the strength of Point 10.

Right away, let me warn you that this point is sometimes a rough one, and that it requires all the brainpower you can give it. But I also want to assure you that it's worth more than the thought and effort it costs.

We've talked about a number of things that will capture a buyer's interest, and we'll talk about still more—but one of the greatest proven sales makers known to man is the simple sentence, "I can give you something you want or need—something that will help you—that you can't get anywhere else." When you say that and back it with proof, you're talking right down your prospect's alley.

There's Always Something

The first reaction of many salesmen—some of them mighty good ones too, is, "But I don't have anything to offer that the customer can't get anywhere else." And that's simply not true. There is *always* something. If you'll just take the trouble to think things out and find it, you'll increase your salespower tremendously. There *has* to be something, whether you realize what it is or not, or you couldn't stay in business.

Did I offer at least one advantage not obtainable elsewhere?

Let me give you a rather far-fetched but true example. The manufacturer of a septic tank—let's be honest, a mildly inferior septic tank—did a healthy business year after year. He had never tried to expand beyond his excellent regional success. He finally decided to branch out—and he didn't even make a small dent in the expanded market. He lost enough money on it so that he gave it up—and rightly so.

You see, in the area where he had been successful, he could offer an advantage that the customer couldn't obtain anywhere else—*much lower shipping costs*. And on this particular item, those shipping costs could amount to real folding money.

Some Variations on a Fine Theme

Now I'd like to tell you about a retail clothing store that sold Palm Beach suits on the "We can give you something you can't get anywhere else" appeal. It was an exclusive men's clothing establishment, catering to men in the high-income brackets.

In the late spring, dealer co-op ads were offered to Palm Beach suit dealers, and in Chicago, the *Tribune*, where I worked at the time, got a lot of that highly desirable advertising.

But the management of this exclusive store said, "We've decided not to run any Palm Beach advertising this year. In the first place, nobody thinks of our store as a place to buy low-priced suits. And we feel that when we run a Palm Beach ad, we just help to create business for all the lower-priced, lower-class stores that are also running ads. It's a Palm Beach suit, regardless of where you buy it, and while the suit is a fine value, we don't get results."

So the *Tribune* brought the "I can give you something you can't get anywhere else" idea into play. The copy and art department prepared a special Palm Beach ad for this exclusive store. It was an attractive ad, in keeping with the store's character, but all the copy said was, "When you buy a Palm Beach suit at this store, you get the same expert alteration and fitting attention that we give on our $175 Name Brand suits—and the price remains a low $00.00."

That store did a phenomenal volume on Palm Beach suits, the most business it had ever done. It's Palm Beach sales were the talk of Chicago merchants—so much so that the following year, a really low-grade store's management said they wanted to do the same kind of thing.

We not only had misgivings about their "I can give you something you can't get anywhere else" approach—we just didn't think it would work.

The approach this store finally took was this, "When you buy a Palm Beach suit here, it will be delivered to you freshly pressed, on a contoured wooden coat hanger."

Nobody else made such an offer, and I'll admit that, much to my surprise, it, too, pulled sensational results. The customers who dealt with this store regarded the offer as a real plus.

Point 10 *always* works. The big question is, how does it apply to you? I remember a session where the salesmen objected loudly and violently that they had no exclusive benefits.

They finally started thinking, and the first suggestions they came up with were pitifully weak. But as they unleashed their minds, they began getting closer and closer to something good. Finally, the sales manager, who had been with the company for nine years, jumped up and said, "I'm absolutely flabbergasted. We have exclusives that I never realized. With this ammunition, we should whip the pants right off of our competition."

It May Be Simple and Obvious

Maybe what you have that the customer can't get anywhere else is something as simple and obvious as the best service warranty, quick delivery, price advantage, longer profit margin, a superior local dealership—but there has to be something.

Remember Lucky Strike's "It's toasted"? I don't know to this day if its exclusive "toasting process" was a benefit, but they certainly sold it as an important one.

Did I offer at least one advantage not obtainable elsewhere?

One television set manufacturer takes a healthy swing at printed circuits and stresses exclusive handcrafted circuitry. Does the exclusive claim work? Well, they're a top company and their stock pays wonderful dividends—and they've featured "exclusives" as long as I can remember.

Once I had a client who had two advertising agencies, one of which I represented. He was in the market to buy some television time, and I wanted the business. So I picked the show I thought best fit his needs and decided to concentrate on it.

Now, ordinarily, television networks are happy to sell their unsponsored shows to any agency that will place the order. He could buy this show from the competing agency just as easily as from us.

24-Hour Option Turned the Trick

So I got a 24-hour option on the program. And I said to the client, "If this is the show you want, and it's certainly the one I'd recommend, I've protected you with an option. Nobody else can offer you this show and nobody else can buy it away from you while the option's in force."

The client said, "Okay—here's your order," and a whopping big sale was made.

Selling for commercial film studios is a rough, fast, hard job. The competition is fierce and sometimes tricky. A film salesman who knew about Point 10 happened to represent a good studio, but one that had relatively little experience in the field of filming commercials. Joe Dee, the salesman, tried and tried to come up with something he could give a prospective customer that the customer couldn't get anywhere else—and nothing he figured out seemed believable to him. His firm hadn't been in the business of making TV commercials long enough to develop much advantage.

Point 10 or not, Joe had to make a sales solicitation on a job that involved a hundred thousand dollars' worth of film, and he wanted that business. About midway through his solicitation, it became painfully apparent to him that he wasn't going to get it. And in the heat of the battle, he came up with one of the most imaginative approaches I've ever seen.

"You can get other studios as large as ours," he said. "You can get some studios with slightly lower prices—although that would frighten me if I were in your place. You can get satisfactory people working on your film—but one thing remains that no other studio can give you, and believe me, with this group of commercials, it's something you need. No other studio can give you Joe Dee!"

The agency television director looked a bit startled. "And just what does that mean to us?" he demanded.

Only Joe Dee Could Do It

Joe took a deep breath. "I'm a film salesman," he answered, "but I've had experience in every phase of the film business. I've worked behind the camera. I know lights. Having been an artist at one stage in my career, I think I know about sets and props. I've done my share of casting. I know how to estimate film costs. I've made a good many bids on commercials.

"And remember this. I've worked with agencies for a good many years. I know what the man who's paying for the film wants. And what makes me the most important part of a job like this, as far as you're concerned, is simply this: I see that you get it! I'll stay right on top of your job from the time it enters the studio through answer prints and finished prints. I doubt if there's another film salesman in the business who will do that for you—and even if he will, I don't think you'll find one with my experience and consequent capability. I'm the guy who'll see that you get a good job—who'll *demand* that you get a good job, and I'm one salesman who knows a good job from a bad one when he sees it.

"Don't think that I'd do this on any little job that came along. There are plenty of routine commercials that don't *need* what I'm offering you. But these commercials aren't routine. They're going to

Did I offer at least one advantage not obtainable elsewhere?

be tricky to do, and twice as tricky to do right. You need me. And the company I represent is the only film studio in the world that can give you my services."

The agency director asked Joe why he thought these particular commercials were tricky, and Joe told him. He explained pitfalls that could be encountered and how they could be avoided.

He added, "I don't know of a film studio in the business that guarantees you'll be satisfied with a job. The quality of a film is a matter of opinion. I've seen agency TV directors who were delighted with jobs I'd have thrown in the cutting-room wastebasket. But I'm completely aware of what you want and I'm good enough to see that you get it. I'm your personal guarantee that this group of commercials will be just the way you want them."

There was more conversation, but Joe got the order. To his credit, he did stay right on top of the job. And the agency man was thoroughly pleased with the end product.

An interesting sidelight is that the film studio itself had no such "exclusive" to offer on jobs that Joe didn't sell. After dropping money on their television commercial operation, they abandoned it and went back to straight show filming, exclusively, where they did have good things in their favor.

When Joe Dee moved to another studio, he kept right on using his version of Point 10—and it continued to work for him.

Another Application of the Point

A fellow who was selling dental equipment called on a young man I know who had just graduated from dental school and was about to set up a specialized practice. This involved buying considerable equipment, and the young dentist was interested in getting that equipment for the lowest possible price.

At least, he was interested until this salesman offered him something he wanted that he couldn't get anywhere else. The salesman said

111

to him, "You say you want the most inexpensive equipment you can get, and I can understand that. But I think there's something else you want. You'd like to acquire a reputation for being a top-notch professional as fast as you can. Right?"

My young friend had to admit that was right. "Very well, then," the salesman continued. "You're going to specialize in an area where you depend on referrals from other dentists. With the training you've had, you should get them. Most dentists don't want to touch the kind of work you hope to do. Now, the equipment I'm selling is the most expensive equipment of its kind on the market—absolutely the most expensive—priced substantially above competitive lines. It has a reputation for being the absolute best. So when you open an office with this equipment, you can almost automatically establish yourself as a top-flight professional who won't have anything but the finest. Every dentist in this community will know what kind of equipment you have, and you can bet your last cent they'll know what it cost. When you buy from my company, you'll get immediate attention and respect that you couldn't get with any other equipment purchase."

He made the sale, and he delivered the benefit that he had promised. My young friend said that other dentists were really impressed, and that he got off to a flying start, where developing the same amount of referral work might otherwise have taken him several years.

That salesman, in my opinion, should win some kind of an award. Instead of trying to overcome high price, he made high price the benefit that the customer couldn't get anywhere else.

I recall a men's clothing salesman who sold a line of suits that was mid-range in both price and quality. He persuaded his company to do a retail survey in an effort to learn who was actually wearing those suits. The survey showed that about 70% of the suits were bought by young men from 21 to 30 years old.

The salesman then began using this sales approach. "You can buy better suits, certainly, and there are much cheaper suits. But you should be interested in getting new customers and keeping them.

"You know that it's virtually impossible to get an older man to

Did I offer at least one advantage not obtainable elsewhere?

change his clothes-buying habits. He's made up his mind what he wants and what he'll spend. New business has to come from young men just getting established in the business or professional worlds.

"Naturally, 70% of our suits are sold to young men from 21 to 30 years old. There's not another line in the United States that sells that high a percentage of its output to that age group—new customers who can become steady customers. If you don't want the business of those young fellows, forget our line—but if you do want it, we can get it for you better than any other line of suits you could carry. We can help you get young men's business more than any other clothing manufacturer in the world."

Remember, there is always some way to come up with a winner on Point 10. If you're puzzled by what it is in your case—well, I told you right at the outset that you'd have to do considerable thinking to get the right applications of the points, didn't I?

But try hard, because Point 10 is the unequalizer that gives you an immediate edge over your competition. When you ask yourself, "Did I offer the customer at least one advantage he could not obtain from any other source?" and the answer is "Yes," you've beaten your competitor.

An Exercise With Point 10

Just for mental exercise, try these:

1. Pick a specific make of television set. What exclusive advantage can you find for it?

2. Choose a specific make of automobile. What exclusive advantage would you sell?

3. Try to find an exclusive advantage in a specific cola soft drink.

4. Try to think of one or more advertising slogans selling an exclusive advantage.

5. What exclusive advantage would you sell in an electric refrigerator you're familiar with (probably the one in your home) ?

11. Did I prove
the endorsement of others
for my product or service?

Yep, you guessed it. This is the testimonial, specific or implied. It's always important, at every level. People are influenced by people they respect, and they're influenced still more by people they both know and respect. Everybody likes to be in good company.

You've heard people laughingly refer to some salesman as a "name dropper." Well, don't join in the laughter, because the salesman who drops the right names at the right times knows what he's doing and makes it pay off.

If a name carries weight and the owner of that name is using your product or service, let the customer know about it. The prospect knows that the Big Name is smart, and his mental reaction is, "I guess if he uses it, it must be pretty good."

Laugh on the Way to the Bank

Many people joke about movie star endorsements of soaps and cosmetics. But the big soap and cosmetic manufacturers who spend millions of dollars on advertising don't laugh. They spend quite a few of those millions on testimonial advertising for only one good reason —because they know it gets results.

When Uncle Will Townsend was selling his checklist of 27 points, the way he threw names around was a caution—and it was all perfectly legitimate and honest, too. He made you feel that you were

Did I prove the endorsement of others?

getting information from a man who hobnobbed with the biggest names in American business. Of course, you couldn't show much doubt or disrespect when he said something—and nobody did.

Many advertisers in recent years have hired what they call a "personality spokesman," a glamorous, known personality who is around to help sell the product. Every sporting goods manufacturer has an "advisory board" or some similar group of top sports personalities. How much advice these people give the manufacturer, I don't know—but they certainly help him to sell his merchandise.

Ted Williams Gear Sells

Ted Williams heads a sporting goods division of one of the world's greatest retailers, and the sports products marketed by this company bear the Ted Williams name. If you were buying an item in sporting goods—be honest, now—which would you buy first, one of the Ted Williams brand or one of the Apex brand?

With so much background in the radio and television business, I had to become acquainted with a good many people who fall into the "celebrity" class. Some of them lose all their glamour and excitement when they get out of the spotlight. Some are nice, quiet people who don't perform at all unless they're on stage. A few are such egotists that a few minutes in their presence is plenty.

But when the conversation is lagging and interest in what I'm trying to sell is at a low ebb, I've found that a true story about a theatrical celebrity immediately wakes up the prospect.

When I was working in a radio-television production office, we received a phone call from a multimillionaire head of a major appliance company. "I'm going to a dinner party Saturday night," he said, "and it's important to me to impress the other guests. What will it cost me to bring a major female movie star in from Hollywood to be my dinner partner? Believe me, all she has to do is be my dinner partner—no funny business of any kind."

115

We called a star who was a friend of ours. She was amused and intrigued by the idea, and demanded a fee of $3,000. The manufacturer accepted it. He called us later to tell us how really delighted he was with the results. "I closed a four-million-dollar deal at that dinner party," he explained. "I had expected these people to try to shove me around a little, and I figured that if I had an important enough dinner partner, they wouldn't dare. I was right."

Remember that the size and importance of a name depends upon who you're talking to. A man who may be nothing at all to the general public may be a dazzling light in the injection molding field. A clubwoman who means nothing at all in New York may be the last social word in Chicago.

Sometimes the names don't have to mean anything to anybody except the man you're selling. The name of another retailer, one who's doing well, can influence the proprietor of a store.

Often, I've seen a salesman on a retail floor make a sale by saying, "Your neighbor, Mrs. Griffin, bought one of these two months ago and she says she wouldn't be without it." I've known dress shops to give very special prices to a few women who are known as style setters in their communities.

A traveling salesman I know who is expected to take his potential client to lunch or dinner never simply asks him. He says, "I'm celebrating, so I'll pop for lunch." Asked what he's celebrating, he says, "I just sold So-and-so (always somebody the potential buyer knows or knows about) the biggest order I ever had from him."

Truth Is Essential

Large orders from firms a prospect respects are always good testimonial selling. But the orders better actually exist, because the man who checks and finds that the order exists only in the mind of the salesman is never going to be a customer.

A cosmetics salesman of my acquaintance is great on figuring out sales gimmicks for retailers. He never takes the credit for them, how-

Did I prove the endorsement of others?

ever. He gets an important outlet to try the new promotion. Then, calling on other customers, he says, "Say, Helen Smith at Bon Ton is using a cute new selling idea. It's boosting sales for her whole department."

The late Biggie Levin had by far the most successful production office in Chicago, and he knew every theatrical celebrity worth knowing (as well as a great many who weren't worth knowing). He had a fiendish trick which never failed to get results, sooner or later. He told anecdotes about himself and specific celebrities that were simply unbelievable. He told them as fact, and you could see raised eyebrows in the conference room or wherever he happened to be. He would always throw in the name of somebody, *not* a celebrity, as having happened to be around when the unbelievable story was alleged to have happened. Sometimes you could almost see the listeners making mental notes of how to reach that person.

They invariably checked, and the story invariably turned out to be completely true. That's what I call putting a double-edge on name dropping.

The Testimony of Satisfied Users

A man who has a reducing-machine franchise in a Midwestern city of about 50,000 population learned that potential buyers were skeptical of the machine's merit. His hardest job was convincing a potential customer that the machine would live up to its claims. After several moderately successful years, he reached the conclusion that the testimony of satisfied users was the most effective selling weapon he could have.

But he didn't rely on the testimony of Hollywood celebrities. He began sending out letters, enclosing self-addressed stamped envelopes for reply, to everyone who had bought one of the machines from him. He sent each letter one year following the addressee's purchase of the machine, and in the letter he asked if the buyer had found the machine effective, if he would recommend it to anyone who was overweight, and if it had lived up to all its advertised claims.

Nearly 80% of the buyers he queried responded to the letter. Well over half of them expressed satisfaction with their purchase and said they would recommend it.

This salesman bought an attractive looseleaf binder and organized the letters by areas of the city and by suburbs and then by nearby towns. It has become a huge book—and he says it does his selling job for him.

"I show the book to every prospect who comes into the salesroom," he told me, "and I take it with me when I make an outside call. I tell prospects that I can't blame them for being skeptical of our claims, and that I'd feel the same way. I give them the book of testimonials and they always start leafing through it. It's not often that they fail to find a letter from someone they know or who at least lives in the same areas as they do. Somehow, that makes the rest of the letters seem more authentic. The letters do a heck of a lot better selling job than I do."

His Most Potent Sales Tool

This man happens to be a real pro salesman, and he's selling an item that requires great salesmanship. He knows a lot about closing, and he's an excellent talker. He's tried every avenue of approach, experimenting to see which will work best. And he is firmly convinced that for the particular thing he's selling, nothing approaches the testimonial letter in sales strength.

A traveling salesman calling on farm equipment dealers pulls out a notebook whenever a dealer says something favorable about the product. "Hey," he says, "I like the way you put that. Do you mind if I write it down just the way you said it?"

Mind? The dealer is flattered. The notebook is alphabetically indexed by counties, and this fellow looks at it between calls. Some time during any call he makes, he introduces a benefit by saying, "You know, I like the way Charlie Johnson, our dealer over at Hastings, expresses it. He says—."

Did I prove the endorsement of others?

And the customer this fellow is trying to sell usually says, "Charlie Johnson? I know him well."

So the salesman follows with, "Do you happen to know Fritz Gerhardt?"

"Sure," the dealer nods. "I've know him for years."

"Well," the salesman says, "Fritz puts the advantages of our line in a little different way. He says—."

And this salesman told me, "Some of the guys razz me about the amount of time I spend on that notebook. But it's worth every minute I've ever given it. I call it my bread-and-butter book."

Tendency to Endorse is Natural

I asked a salesman of office equipment if he had any difficulty getting testimonials, thinking I might get a story of adroit maneuvering.

"No trouble at all," he told me. "Easy as shooting fish in a barrel."

"What's your technique?" I asked him.

"I tell the customer I'd like to have a testimonial from him," he said. "He's always kind of flattered. He thinks of testimonials in connection with Big Name celebrities, and it seems to him that maybe my company thinks he's a celebrity in his line of business. The testimonial is always good, too. He's bought the product and is using it. He isn't going to say, 'When I bought this stuff, the salesman sure made a patsy of me. I really got hooked. It's no good but I was stupid enough to get stuck with it.' What he says will reveal that he showed his usual good judgment."

There's been a tendency in recent years to minimize the importance of the testimonial—which is too bad. It has happened because some of the testimonials used in advertising have been so stupidly unbelievable. And I'll certainly go along with the premise that the unbelievable testimonial is no good. For that matter, an unbelievable *any*thing is no good in selling.

The honest endorsement of others for your product or service, however, still carries real weight and can be a great help in making sales.

Are there good testimonials available for your product or service? If not, where can you get them and how?

When you answer yes to the question, "Did I prove the endorsement of others for my product or service?," you're backing up your own claims with the word of disinterested parties whose word carries weight.

12. Did I use
my firm's sales aids
to the best advantage?

If you don't use your firm's sales aids to the best advantage, you're making your job harder than it needs to be.

This point deals with sales manuals, special literature, displays, merchandising packages, demonstration kits—every tool that you are given and expected to use as a salesman.

Let me say first that I've seen sales aids foisted upon salesmen that no really professional salesman would even dream of using. Some of these things cost plenty of money, too. I've seen some canned sales presentations that may have been just great in the sales manager's hands, but which made certain of his men look like blithering idiots.

"A Tasty Tidbit of Selling Succulence"

Never will I forget a convention I attended where the sales manager went through a new easel presentation for his men to use, a flip-chart prepared at enormous cost. The third page had nothing on it but this: "Here's a tasty tidbit of selling succulence." I *knew* the salesmen this book was to be used by, and I couldn't imagine one man in the group being able to force those words out of his mouth without gagging.

Another memory that stands out is that of a furnace manufacturer who equipped his men with a cutaway cross-section of the works of the furnace, cleverly engineered so that moving parts could be made to work. The salesmen didn't happen to be engineers, and the men

121

they were calling on were plumbing-and-heating shopowners. The thing was so complicated that nobody could possibly use it effectively.

Much as I hate to admit it, there is a great deal of pitifully bad sales material put into the hands of salesmen by companies who should know better.

Let's assume, however, that your firm knows what it's doing and that it is furnishing you with the finest sales tools you could have. You'd be shocked at the number of salesmen who have great sales tools and simply don't take the trouble to use them.

I've known salesmen who were given beautiful presentations on superb merchandising packages designed by their company who didn't even mention the merchandising plan to their customers. Their explanation to me was that they didn't want to ask their customers for that extra money required. Actually, these salesmen were doing their customers a disfavor, because those merchandising packages had only one purpose—to move the merchandise out of the customer's store.

A kitchen manufacturer once had me prepare an easel presentation to quality department stores. The purpose of the presentation was to persuade the department store to invest $12,000 in a model-kitchen setup. I thought the whole presentation made plenty of sense and that it would do the job. Executives of the company thought so, too. But the salesmen weren't quite so enthusiastic.

First Approach Successful

The head of the company asked me to do him a favor. "We've set up the first appointment in St. Louis, at a store whose business can be of tremendous importance to us. Our salesman in that territory hasn't given the presentation and I wonder if you'd do it, with him simply going along as an observer?"

I agreed to do it, went to St. Louis, and the deal was closed in about an hour and a half.

Did I use my firm's sales aids to best advantage?

A few days later, I got another call from the head of the company. "We've set up an appointment in Detroit," he explained, "and our salesman in that territory is scared to death he'll blow it. You closed St. Louis, so I wonder if you'd make another trip—to Detroit. Let our man there see how this works."

I agreed—a bit more reluctantly, this time. And the sale in Detroit was just as easy to make as the one in St. Louis.

Then the following week, the company head called again. "The next appointment," he said, "is in Chicago. Since you're already there, it wouldn't be too much trouble or take too much of your time to do this again, would it?"

Salesmen Still Reluctant

I agreed—a *lot* more reluctantly, this time, and again we got almost instant results.

The following week, the kitchen manufacturer called again. "We have an appointment set up in Denver," he said, and I didn't let him get any further. "You can go straight to hell," I told him. "If I wanted to be a salesman for your company, I'd apply for a job with you." He admitted, cheerfully, that what he'd been asking might have been unreasonable and said I wouldn't have to go to Denver.

The terrible thing, though, was that the salesmen never did use that beautiful, carefully prepared presentation. Why? They choked up. The thought of asking $12,000 for a floor display unit was more than they could take. They not only couldn't believe that their management knew what it was doing but refused to give it a trial.

One salesman in a stove company sold thousands of beautiful booklets to nearly every customer in his territory. Not one other man sold *any* of the booklets the first time around.

Here's how the one fellow did it. He took a rough layout of the booklet and typewritten copy with him. He went in to a customer and said, "Bill, we've worked out an idea for a booklet for you that should sell a lot of ranges for you. It really has what it takes." The customer agreed that there was plenty of sell in the copy, but said that the booklet would cost too much.

"How much do you figure it would cost?" the salesman asked.

"Oh, a booklet like that, in color, would probably cost me at least a nickel apiece." the customer answered.

"No, sir," the salesman said, whipping out one of the booklets. "Here it is, and I can deliver it to you with imprint for $5 a thousand —half a cent a booklet."

He sold booklets that in turn sold gas ranges. His fellow salesmen didn't.

The Chicago distributor for a good line of automobile additives remembered a slidefilm that the parent film had made in the dim past, and it had sold a lot of merchandise. He wanted more things like it, and they weren't forthcoming.

So he made a slidefilm of his own—on a radiator stop-leak. He equipped his salesmen with a few DuKane countertop slidefilm projectors—and business rolled in to the point where the manufacturer bought the slidefilm from him to use in other markets.

A good salesman not only carries his firm's sales tools, but he studies them. He finds new ways to use them. He doesn't complain about carrying the material because he knows that the company's only purpose in developing it was to increase sales.

Training With Sales Aids Necessary

Some companies have had so much trouble getting good salesmen that they depend less and less upon the men and more and more upon the sales tools they give to them. On sheer weight—given a large number of men in the field—this seems to work out. Honestly, though, the kind of men these companies have at the bottom of their lists are salesmen I wouldn't hire for $10 a week.

124

Did I use my firm's sales aids to best advantage?

Several good companies for whom I've done sales training had really excellent selling tools for their men. But they wrongly took it for granted that the men would know how to use the materials. To increase one firm's sales sharply, all that had to be done was to hold a one-day training session to show the men how the material should be used.

The commonest failure to use company sales tools to the best advantage is the salesman's failure to capitalize on his company's advertising. In some companies, the salesmen actually ignore company advertising, and I've seen instances where they sold *against* it. These were instances where the sales manager and the advertising manager fought each other instead of cooperating.

Advertising a Friend, Not a Rival

One Midwestern company that comes to mind spends about three million dollars a year on its advertising—and the advertising is good. The sales manager feels that he should have another $500,000 a year for his sales department. I don't know whether he has deliberately instructed his salesmen to ignore company advertising or not, but I do know that the men never mention it in their sales solicitations— and the features and benefits the salesmen talk about to their customers are not the ones that are being emphasized in the advertising.

If you are selling to retailers or jobbers, a good company advertising program can be one of the most potent sales weapons in your arsenal.

Many retailers and jobbers feel that they are forced to stock a well-advertised item whether they want to or not. They know that good advertising will move the goods into the hands of the consumer, and they feel that the risk of being stuck with a load of dead merchandise is infinitesimal as long as the advertising program continues.

Many a manufacturer who found his men unable to sell a large chain has instituted a heavy television and newspaper advertising campaign in the chain's area and has forced the chain to stock its product.

When a good sales manager holds a sales meeting, he has somebody from his advertising agency there to inform his men about coming advertising. The men get tearsheets or proofs of the ads. They get the circulation of the newspapers and magazines, the locations of the billboards, and traffic figures—the ratings of television and radio shows with the number of homes reached, a breakdown of audience composition, and the frequency of impression. The men are shown how to sell that information to their customers.

A good retailer nearly always ties in with national advertising—but too often fails to tell his people on the floor how *they* should tie in with it. Most retail salesmen are free to admit that it's much easier to sell nationally advertised and locally advertised products than it is to sell anything that doesn't have that advertising behind it.

We were shopping for a new mattress. A salesman in one store said, "This is the special that's being featured in this week's issue of *Life*." He showed us the ad and pointed out some of the things the ad said about the mattress. We bought that mattress. The interesting thing, however, is that we had just seen the same mattress in another store. The salesman in that store had said, "This is a good mattress and we're running a special on it." Somehow, we hadn't been impressed.

For many salesmen, a good advertising campaign in industrial or trade publications conditions his prospects so that his selling job is greatly simplified—*if* he follows up the information that has been stressed in the trade ads, amplifies it, and asks for the order.

Taking a Lesson From P&G

Some salesmen take a perverse pride in never mentioning the benefits that are featured in their company's advertising. Perhaps they need to get into other approaches to sell a specific customer, but to completely ignore a preconditioning job that has been done for them seems just plain stupid.

Proctor and Gamble salesmen, who seem to be uniformly bright, alert, well informed and well trained, all do a fine job of selling their

Did I use my firm's sales aids to best advantage?

company's advertising along with the merchandise. Listen to one of them talking to a customer about P&G advertising and you see what an effective sales tool a company's advertising program can be.

When a drug company is introducing a new proprietary, it's common practice for the salesman, trying to get the new product on the druggist's shelf, to offer a local advertising campaign if a substantial order is closed. More often than not in these cases, it's the advertising that tips the scale and induces the druggist to buy.

One cosmetics salesman admitted to me, "With all the lines trying to get in and get display in every outlet, I'd be absolutely helpless without our company's advertising program. I find myself selling the advertising harder than I sell the line. Maybe my boss wouldn't like that, but it works—and he won't complain as long as I keep bringing in the orders."

Charge Salesmen for Ad Leads

An encyclopedia publisher runs coupon ads and charges its salesmen $2.50 for each lead secured from the advertising. "There was a time," they say, "when we gave the leads to the men. We found out that they weren't following through and the leads were being wasted. Once they started paying for the leads, their attitude changed. Now, they follow through fast, and when they get a bad lead, they yell bloody murder."

Maybe if more salesmen had to pay something for their company's advertising, they'd do a better job of capitalizing on it. When you think about mail-order advertising's ability to sell without any outside help, you wonder why any salesman would ignore the aid his company has given him.

Whatever sales tools your organization furnishes must be adapted to your personality and sales approach. And in the opinion of the men who put the Dartnell/Anderson 20 Point System together, you make a grave mistake when you depend almost entirely on prefabricated tools. That makes you little more than a messenger boy.

Some sales departments don't have much idea of how their men are using their preplanned material. A book publisher says that any salesman who uses the company's canned material as instructed will earn $20,000 a year. As proof, they point to certain men who are making at least that much money. A little research on their men shows that it is *not* the top men who are depending entirely on tools, but the *bottom* men. The top moneymakers are excellent professional salesmen who have developed a great many stratagems—some of which, incidentally, would make management cringe.

There should be ways to make your company's sales tools help you —ways to use them generally and ways for specific situations.

Putting Some Points to Work

Before we move on to the Opposition Points, try to apply Points 6 through 12 to your specific selling job:

Point 6. How can you best convey the background and merits of the company you represent? Do you need to sell yourself harder on this point? What are the greatest things in favor of your company? Do you know all you need to know about company policy and the organization's standing in its industry?

Point 7. What new, beneficial thing about the product or service you're selling will do you the most good in making sales? Is there honestly anything new for you to talk about? If not, what new slant should you take on a beneficial thing the prospect already knows about? How can you put news value into your selling approach? Is it inherent in the product or service or in an application?

Point 8. Was the customer thoroughly acquainted with all of the advantages of your product or service by the time you concluded your solicitation? Did you do enough probing to find out where he was well informed and where he wasn't? Were you a good listener? Did you unnecessarily overdo your product information part of the presentation, spending too much time on things he already knew? Do you have a concise, well-worded list of all the advantages you can offer? Have

Did I use my firm's sales aids to best advantage?

you weighed their relative importance? Are the benefits you're using to sell your product or service believable?

Point 9. How can you get the customer to participate in your sales presentation? Do you have a good product or service demonstration? Do you know how to use it to the best advantage? Is there any way to make it more dramatic and more effective? Are you missing any ways of getting your prospective customer to participate in both the demonstration and your presentation?

Point 10. What advantage can you offer the customer that he can't obtain from any other source? Is there more than one? Do you know *all* your exclusive benefits? Is there any way you can stress your exclusive advantages by what you say or do?

Quote the Man Who Owns One

Point 11. Are there people who use your product or service whose endorsement can help you to make sales? Do you keep full information on them? Are you making the most of satisfied customers in your sales area?

Point 12. Can you determine any ways to use your company's sales aids to better advantage? Are you making full use of the tools your company gives you? Can you capitalize on your company's advertising better than you've been doing?

Remember, there are salesmen who rely on nothing but the Proof Points to make sales. Are you using them primarily as justification on the buyer's part or as reason? Perhaps they can both justify a purchase and be the reason for it. Never underestimate their importance. And whenever you can, study successful mail-order advertising to see how effective carefully worded proof points can be.

Opposition To A Sale

Somewhere, some time, some great salesman is going to make a sale without encountering any opposition. Logic says it has to happen. But of the six sales managers who participated in the planning of the 20-Point System, not one remembers it ever happening to him, and I've never seen it happen to anyone else.

The sales manager I've dubbed "The Personality Kid" says of Opposition, "This is the part of selling where the 'canned' presentation falls right on its face and the fate of the sale rests in the hands of the salesman. It's where ad-libbing becomes a fine art."

It is also the part of the sale where the salesman must be much more adroit than the advertising copywriter. The salesman faces the same thing that the debater does in what debaters call the rebuttal—but he must be faster, smoother, and more tactful than any debater.

The debater's job is to sell the audience into believing that he's right and his opponent is wrong. The worse he can make his opponent look, the better he looks.

That's not so at all in making a sale. The only person you have to sell is the one who's raising the objections. Even questioning his statements can make him so angry that the sales solicitation may be all over. It's not too difficult to prove to a prospective customer that he doesn't know what he's talking about—but if you can think of any harder task than selling him after you've proved him to be an idiot, let me know what it is.

130

When I began selling, I usually answered objections by saying, "Oh, but you're wrong." Since I was a teenager and the potential customers were much older, the antagonism was compounded.

Finally, thank goodness, I went on a sales solicitation with the great Hugh Hogan, and I learned one of the greatest lessons about selling that I've ever run across. If you don't already know it, you're going to get your money's worth right now, in a few words.

Hugh's customer was obnoxious and cantankerous. I've never heard more opposition, more objectionably worded. I stood in open-mouthed indignation, waiting for Hugh to give me the signal to leave with him. But the signal didn't come.

Hugh was ordinarily a high-pressure salesman who worked to close a sale and leave as quickly as he could. But on this occasion, I've never seen greater patience, tolerance, and charm. I wondered secretly if Hugh had some extra time to kill and wanted to see how far the prospect would go. As far as making a sale was concerned, it didn't seem to me that there was the remotest chance.

The clash went on and on—and on. Calling it a clash isn't quite right, because Hugh never lost his temper, which I thought he had every right to do.

Finally, Hugh said, "Well, Mr. Call, it looks like all the difficulties are ironed out. Actually, we're in complete agreement, right?"

"I guess so," the customer mumbled.

A Quick Surrender—Why?

"In that case," Hugh whipped out an order blank, "it's the proper time for you to sign an order."

You could have knocked me over *without* a feather. Mr. Call signed his name to the order blank with a flourish, shook hands with Hugh, and walked with us to the door, affable for the first time in over an hour that we'd been with him.

When we reached the street, I said, "Hugh, I'd have bet anything I had that Mr. Call wasn't going to give you an order. I thought you were wasting your time."

"Why in the world did you think that?" he asked, in genuine astonishment.

"Because of the rough, tough time he gave you, every step of the way. All those objections."

Hugh was even more astonished. "Kid," he said, "you have a lot to learn about selling. When a customer *doesn't* give you any argument is the time to worry. The more he argues and the more he objects, the surer you are of a sale—that is, if you know what you're doing."

I shook my head. "I don't get it."

Why Opposition Is Good

Hugh smiled at me tolerantly. "Kid," he explained, "a man only argues if he's interested—if he cares."

And Hugh Hogan was absolutely right, as I later proved to myself on many a sales call for many years.

When I ask you to exchange your money for my goods or services, making you want what I'm selling isn't quite enough. You want to be absolutely sure you're doing the right thing in buying. To assure yourself, you come up with every objection you can think of—maybe some you don't even think are valid. You want me to reassure you that you're making a smart purchase and prove to you that you're right in buying from me.

If I haven't turned you on at all, if I've failed to arouse any desire on your part, you won't bother with opposition. The chances are that you'll simply say, "Sorry, I'm not interested." That little comment has been the sad obituary on many a sales presentation.

Over the years, I've been astonished at the number of really good salesmen who had never realized that opposition was a step in the right direction, until it was pointed out to them. Once they began thinking about it, they all admitted that it was true—and unanimously agreed that the toughest customer there is in the world is old Mum's-the-Word, the fellow who never voices any opposition.

And when you run across the Silent Type, don't blame him. The problem isn't his but yours. You haven't made him care enough about what you're selling to come up with any opposition. You haven't even captured his interest, let alone whetted his desire.

There are cases where a prospect comes into contact with you with his mind already made up to buy—but I've never known of a case where you really *sell* anything without some opposition.

I asked Hugh Hogan why his argumentative customer had asked so *many* questions and brought up so many really asinine points of contention.

"Because I had been in too much of a hurry and had done a perfectly stinking job of selling," Hugh admitted. "A sensible buyer," he said, "gives you opposition as long as there's a single thing about your product he doesn't quite understand."

"And don't feel badly about opposition or let it worry you, kid," he added with a grin. "If it weren't for the opposition, who would need salesmen?"

Without It, Who'd Need Salesmen?

The sales manager I call The Roughneck says, "I used to worry myself sick about objections. I thought you had to be a great ad-libber to answer unexpected beefs that customers might throw at you at any time, right out of the blue. I finally got smart when I watched a good encyclopedia salesman at work. This fellow, I happened to know, couldn't ad-lib his way out of a paper bag—but he didn't need to, because he had carefully worked out a darned near perfect answer to every objection that a prospect could throw at him. Watching him work on four different calls, I caught on to the fact that his answers were almost uniform. Right away, I began thinking about the objections I'd been fumbling around handling, and trying to work out some sensible answers to them. Once I got 'em set, taking care of objections was a breeze."

The Boy Wonder had gone through a quite different problem with opposition. "On my first real selling job," he says, "the company told us what the opposition would be and gave us what they thought were good answers. The only trouble was, the answers weren't my kind of talk and the logic didn't seem solid to me. I had to rewrite them to keep them from sounding like they were automatic and to make them sound sensible to me. Some of the men used the answers right out of the training course, word for word. They seemed to do all right, but they sounded like robots to me. I couldn't have done it."

The Competitor says, "I had a sales manager who was a lulu. There were two objections to our product that nobody had a good answer for. We kept throwing the objections at him, and all he did was get madder and madder at us. 'If you guys were any good, you wouldn't have to come to me to bail you out,' he told us. "I don't know of any product that's perfect. It's your job to sell in spite of those two objections.' Well, we *didn't* sell, because one of our competitors knew how to make the most of our shortcomings. It took the company two years to make up its mind to change the product to answer the objections— but I wasn't there by that time. I had decided that any company that could ignore such shortcomings wasn't the place for me."

Perhaps Proof Points Need Reviewing

There is no more difficult part of a sales solicitation than answering the opposition the customer throws at you. You can't ever be sure what it's going to be and you never know when it's coming.

While it's difficult, it's also extremely helpful, because it's from customer opposition that you learn what direction you should take. You also learn where you've failed to make yourself clear. The objections a customer raises give you a second chance on proof points you've slighted.

More salesmen get thrown by objections than by any other part of the sales presentation—usually because the opposition upsets them. It's unexpected and it interrupts the sales solicitation. The only time you should let it upset you is when you can't handle it. In such an instance, you *should* be upset and should start immediately to correct what has to be a bad weakness in your presentation. But at least wait until you're away from the prospect before you show your feelings.

The Competitor says, "When I'm interviewing men for sales jobs, they try to sell me on hiring them, naturally. And I throw objections at them every step of the interview. They probably think I'm pretty miserable—but they'll run up against some tough cookies once they come to work for our company, and I'm interested in seeing how well they can handle unexpected objections. I look more for their ability to field opposition than for any other single thing. The man who can answer or offset objections without antagonizing a customer can handle just about any selling problem there is. When I find such a fellow, I grab him."

Don't Choke Up!

Whatever you do, don't panic or choke up when opposition comes hard and fast. Remember Hugh Hogan's observation that a prospect only offers objections when he's interested—when he cares. Think to yourself, "Now I'm getting somewhere. All I have to do is answer these questions satisfactorily and I'm going to close a sale."

If you can do this, you'll be a real pro. The "hunch" salesman gives up when the going gets rocky—and he walks away from the prospect firm in the belief that the man wasn't really a prospect at all. Opposition doesn't lead him to improve his sales presentation a bit. Indeed, he doesn't ever get the idea that there was anything wrong with it.

13. Did I overcome customer objection without encouraging an argument?

You shouldn't be surprised when you run into opposition. It's natural and usual. Accept it, and accept that part of your job is to overcome it.

Before you can overcome it, though, you have to find out why the opposition exists.

One common reason for opposition is that the potential customer doesn't understand all he should about the product or service you're selling. That's your fault, not his, and he's doing you a favor by giving you the opportunity to increase his knowledge.

Then again, maybe he does understand your product or service, but you haven't translated it into benefits that appeal to him. He can see that what you're selling has physical merit, but he can't see any good reason why he should buy it. You have to make him want it before you can get him to put out his money for it.

Price Objections May Be Phony

Sometimes, the objections that are voiced aren't really the right ones. It's easy to say, "It's too high-priced," for example—whether you think it is or not—and it's extremely difficult to say, "The boss says I should buy anything in this line from his second cousin, who works for your competitor."

Price, of course, is one of the most commonly voiced objections—and it's *nearly* always one of the easiest to overcome.

Did I overcome objections without encouraging argument?

The soundest opposition comes from lack of knowledge about a certain benefit or physical feature. Objecting is a much easier way to get additional information than admitting your ignorance.

Another reason for opposition is that you haven't gotten the customer with you when you were on the Proof Points and should have encouraged him to agree with you. You'll seldom find a customer who'll admit that he doesn't understand one of the proof points. He'll say nothing, but then later, watch out—he'll give you opposition on it.

Fairly often, opposition will come on a competitor's "exclusive" feature. Your prospect has read about it, or another salesman has sold him on it—and it's something you don't have.

Objections Most Often Heard

Sometimes, you'll get opposition because you're not talking the customer's language. Maybe you're in too much of a hurry. Maybe you haven't taken his viewpoint.

Opposition may come because the customer just plain doesn't like you or your company. There has to be a reason for that dislike, and you have to find out what it is before you can correct it.

Of the 12 points in the 20 Point list already covered, I'd say that objections most often stem from these:

Point 1—Did I make a favorable impression on the customer?

Point 2—Did I talk from the customer's viewpoint?

Point 3—Did I find the basic desire or need on the part of the customer and then capitalize on it?

Point 6—Did I properly convey the background and merits of the company?

Point 8—Was the customer thoroughly acquainted with *all* the advantages of the product or service by the time I concluded my solicitation?

Whatever the opposition is, you must find out why it exists. How do you do it? Ask. And get him to tell you whether you're right or wrong in what you think his objection is.

Then answer the objection. But answer it without arguing.

Winning an argument with a customer is almost synonymous with losing a sale. The temptation to tell a customer off is always an expensive one to gratify.

I've never forgotten Harry Briggs, who had the prime accounts on a newspaper. First, he won a knock-down-and-drag-out argument with the advertising manager of the best department store in the city. The next day, the store management requested that Mr. Briggs be replaced as the salesman. The newspaper, wanting to hold the store's business, had no choice.

About a month later, Harry had a row with another of his good accounts, and he won that argument, too. Again, the account asked for a new man to handle its business.

Within a year, Harry Briggs had been taken off every good account he'd handled. The paper reluctantly let him go.

And Harry said in parting, "I have no regrets for anything I've done. I was right in every argument I had, and what's more, I made every one of them admit that I was right."

Won the Arguments, Lost the Job

Sure, he did. He won the arguments and lost his job. The saddest part of his story is that he didn't learn a thing from what happened to him. I understand that he still has just as big a chip on his shoulder as he ever had.

Every sensible salesman knows that it's silly to get into arguments with customers—but how do you stop opposition *without* argument?

 I had the pleasure of watching an automobile salesman work to sell a couple a car—a particular car, a demonstrator that the dealer

Did I overcome objections without encouraging argument?

wanted to clear out in order to buy new demonstrators. Everything went along beautifully until the wife said, "I don't like the color. I wouldn't have it!"

The salesman was good. He said, "Maybe I shouldn't tell you this, but I disliked the color violently when this car came in. I thought it was terrible. The factory man said they'd had other complaints. You see, it's a brand new color that nobody's familiar with, yet. The factory has the assurance of its designers that this particular color is going to be the hot color in women's fashions this fall, the newest and smartest thing. Even so, it was a little far out for a conservative, middle-aged boy like me. But I understand that in New York, it's the color most in demand. I guess the young fashion setters have come out in favor of it and everybody's trying to get on the bandwagon early.

The "Yes, But" Technique

"I guess they know what they're doing, because I'll have to admit that the color has grown on me. Conservative as I am, I've come to like it in spite of myself. Even a stodgy guy like me pays more attention to fashion than he'd like to admit, and I guess I must have a secret longing to dig the smart, new things."

The woman eyed the car critically. "You know," she said, "I think I like it a little better, just standing here looking at it. It sort of grows on you, know what I mean?"

"I certainly do," the salesman nodded, "because that's exactly what happened in my case."

This salesman used the "Yes, but" technique, and used it masterfully. He didn't seem to be disagreeing with the woman at all, but he sized her up right and knew that what he was saying would sell her away from her opposition.

When I was buying my first electric organ, I knew what make I really wanted—but another considerably lower-priced one had much flashier percussion effects. The demonstrator could make it sound like

139

a steel guitar, a banjo, a xylophone—you name it, and he could duplicate the effect.

The organ I really wanted had much less to offer in the way of percussion effects, and I told the salesman so.

"That's quite true," the salesman agreed. "The Brand X organ does have some mighty tricky percussion effects. It even has some that I've never seen called for in any piece of music. For that matter, have you ever thought about how seldom percussion effects are used in organ music? Think of any top organist you've heard, and tell me, do you remember his or her having used much percussion?"

I tried to recall, and had to admit that I couldn't think of any.

"That's good," the salesman nodded, "because so many people buying their first organ don't realize what they'll be doing with it after they get it. They don't stop to think that percussion is more or less of a gimmick—great for a tricky demonstration but not of much use when you sit down to play. I try to tell them that the occasions when they'll use percussion are few and far between—but unlike you, they don't realize it. And this organ right here, the one you want, has more than enough percussion to fill your needs. I daresay you'll never ever once use all the percussion settings you can get with it. You'll be interested in playing music as it's supposed to be played, not in coming up with freak sounds.

Counterbalancing the Benefits

"And of course, the Brand X organ has one problem that all organs except the one right here have—it gets out of tune. When it gets even slightly out of tune, anybody with your knowledge of music will feel that it has to be tuned, which costs money. Because of the way this organ is designed, because of its basic idea, it never has to be tuned. It can't get out of tune. Don't you agree that this feature will be far more important to you than gimmick percussion?"

And I said that I certainly did agree.

Did I overcome objections without encouraging argument?

This salesman used a combination of the "yes, but" technique and counterbalancing benefits, pointing out a feature that counterbalances the objection. He not only made me admit the error of my opposition but made me feel that I was a pretty smart fellow in acknowledging it.

If there's an objection you honestly can't answer, the counterbalancing benefit is often your best solution to the problem.

Some salesmen recognize the existence of objections to what they're selling and use the great technique of not just acknowledging but actually pointing out those objections before the customer mentions them. They answer the objection or counterbalance it before it has become an issue.

An Advance Man's Strategy

When I was driving automobiles "blindfolded" as a newspaper exploitation stunt, I hired an advance man to help with the selling job. I thought he was doing a great job, until customers began telling me what a pitifully poor salesman he was.

"You ought to get rid of that fellow," one automobile dealer told me. "He doesn't know the first thing about selling."

A newspaper advertising manager told me virtually the same thing. The catch was that he had sold both of these men, and sold them on a basis that was highly profitable for me.

After hearing complaints about his weak salesmanship for a few weeks, my curiosity was aroused to the point where I decided to make a few calls with him.

I was shocked on the first call. The car dealer was the key man in each blindfold-drive stunt. He rightly paid the most for it, and you really had no promotion to sell others until you'd sold him.

My advance man said to this car dealer, "Let's start right out by my admitting that this is stunt advertising. I don't know what you think about stunt advertising, but I think a lot of it is bad. It seems to attract a type of person who's what I'd call hit-and-run—people who are only interested in getting your money and then getting out of town as fast as they can.

"These people come in with a stunt and they make extravagant promises without having the faintest intention of fulfilling them. At least, they don't know that they *can* fulfill them.

"I'd be insulting your intelligence if I told you that taking part in this promotion would sell 20 cars for you—or 15 cars—even one car. I don't know whether it will or not. There's no way for you to know in advance, either.

"I do know this. You won't do much selling while the stunt is in progress, because everybody in your community will be focusing on the blindfold drive. People will want to watch it rather than listen to any sales talk.

"We won't make promises we can't fulfill. Even if we wanted to do it, your newspaper, the one that's sponsoring the blindfold drive, wouldn't let us. They expect to be doing business with you for a long time, and they don't want to earn your enmity.

Only Two Guarantees

"We guarantee to do only two things, really—to get you six days of front-page newspaper publicity and to make your car the focal point of all eyes on the day of the drive. You should get the largest crowd to your showroom for the start of the drive that you've ever had. They'll see your various models. They'll see you and your salesmen. And after George has been blindfolded by the mayor, before he starts the drive, he'll give that crowd a demonstration of the car's features such as you've never seen. He knows the sales manual on your car from cover to cover—and he'll point out the features to the crowd while he's blindfolded. They'll be getting a great sales presentation without realizing it. They'll think of what's happening as entertainment.

"Then, when the drive starts, your car will be the center of attention in the business district for 8 hours. At the finish of the drive,

Did I overcome objections without encouraging argument?

he'll pull a big crowd back to your showroom. And he'll tell that crowd what a pleasure it was to drive the car, inviting them to let you set up a demonstration ride for them.

"Remember, all we guarantee to do is get you the most publicity you've ever had, and to draw a crowd which will be given a sales talk on your car. If we guarantee anything else, we're either guessing or lying."

I couldn't believe it. He had deliberately brought up the arguments I had been trying to avoid without success. "I don't believe in stunt advertising" and "This won't bring in a dime's worth of business."

His Sales Were "Clean"

But he didn't get those objections. He brought them up, himself. He didn't try to deny their validity, because he couldn't. He agreed that the objections were there. But when he began telling about what we could do for the car dealer, his believability was complete.

He used "Yes, but" and counterbalancing benefits, but he brought up the opposition, himself, and got it out of the way before it became a problem.

All that summer, people who bought the drive confided in me what a poor salesman my advance man was—and I didn't change him because he was making sales—much cleaner sales, I might add, than most stunt salesmen get.

Sometimes it's possible to reword an objection so that it seems to answer itself. On many an occasion, I've pretended not to understand an objection. "I want to get this clear in my mind," I say. "I don't think you mean that you can't afford it, because it seems to me that it will cost you far more *not* to have this than to have it. I've explained to you the savings that this service will make for you. And it simply has to get you some extra business. When you consider that it may save you as much as $500 a month on engravings, the price of $50 a month isn't really an expenditure. It's cutting a present cost. Perhaps what you mean is that the price is higher than that of some other service. But you must not mean that, either, because the services are all priced within a few dollars of each other and this one offers a good many more features than the others. I want to be sure I get this straight. Exactly what *is* your objection?"

Price objections are so common that most salesmen already have ways of handling them.

A salesman who had been offered a drink in the prospect's office before they went to lunch noticed that the man had a bottle of Old Fitzgerald and a bottle of Chivas Regal in his desk.

At lunch, the prospect said, "You've got a good line, Mac, but your price is too high."

"Thanks," Mac answered. "I mean thanks for saying that I have a good line. Do you think the *quality* is too high?"

"The quality can't be too high, as far as I'm concerned," the prospect said.

"I'm glad you feel that way about it," Mac nodded. "Some people don't. It's always been my experience that you pay less for quality in the long run than for anything else you buy."

"What do you mean by that?" the customer asked.

An Example of Good Value

"Figure the cost of a Steinway piano over a lifetime," the salesman explained. "Then figure the difference in what you get in a Steinway and what you get in a cheap piano. The extra cost per year isn't much, and if you're a musician, what you get out of it is plenty. I know you feel the same way I do about how little you pay for top quality over inferior products."

"Yeah? How do you know that?" the customer demanded.

"Because you were nice enough to invite me into your office for a drink before we went to lunch," the salesman answered. "And you had two bottles of liquor in your desk—a bottle of Old Fitzgerald and

Did I overcome objections without encouraging argument?

a bottle of Chivas Regal. You could have had a bottle of cut-rate bourbon and a bottle of cheap Scotch. Let's take the bottle of Old Fitzgerald. You could have bought a bottle of bourbon for a dollar less, but you didn't—and I don't, either, because I figured out that I pour 16 or 17 drinks from a bottle. That means that I pay about six cents more per drink if I pour good stuff. I flatter the people I serve. They know that I think enough of them to serve good liquor. And my guests and I get considerably more than six cents' worth of pleasure out of a really good drink."

Painless and Personal

"You're absolutely right," the prospect said. "You should see some of the slop that my friends serve when I go to their homes. I wouldn't serve it to a bum, let alone a friend. They never seem to get the idea that good liquor costs so little more than bad. Yessir, you've got a good point."

That was both a painless and personal way of overcoming the objection, "Your prices are too high."

"I can't afford it right now" is something else. It may be that the prospect actually can't afford the expenditure at the moment. It may also be that he thinks the price is too high or that this is simply his simplest and easiest way of getting rid of you.

A salesman who was selling thousand-dollar coffee urns to restaurants and institutions had a restaurant proprietor say to him, "It's the best coffee urn I've ever seen, I'll admit that—but, darn it, I can't afford it."

The salesman nodded agreement. "That may be true," he said. "A thousand dollars is a lot to invest in a coffee urn. But I just used a word to thing about—invest. Good coffee is one of the most important things there is in the restaurant business. The reputation for serving a good cup of coffee always pays off. Now, you have the best restaurant in this community, but you're getting more competition every month because you're in a boom town. Two new restaurants have ordered this equipment. They don't think of it as an expense but as

145

an investment. They want to get the reputation for serving a good cup of coffee as fast as they can. You've seen how this urn will save you money. Figured over a three-year period—and you can have that long to pay for it under our special plan—the cost of the stale coffee you now throw away every day—a cost which this urn can eliminate —probably amounts to more than the payments.

"And there's another thing you have to consider. It's nice for you that you do have to consider it. You're the Number one restaurant man in this town, no question about it. Can you afford to have two new restaurants open with coffee equipment that's better than yours? Can you afford not to keep ahead of competition in every way, just as you always have? Can you afford to let another restaurant have something newer and better in any department than you have?"

Key phrases here that kept the prospect from getting miffed were: "You're the Number One restaurant man in this town" and "Can you afford not to keep ahead of competition in every way, just as you always have?"

Self-Examination on Point 13

Any customer has to enjoy that way of overcoming his objection.

What are the commonest objections you can expect in selling your product or service?

Name an objection that would indicate you have fallen down on a personal or proof point.

Do you have a good answer for any objection you might encounter? If there isn't a good answer for one, do you have a good counterbalance, something to make up for the objection?

How can you best use the "Yes, but" technique?

Work out ways of using every technique without getting into arguments.

Remember that while opposition always indicates interest, you must overcome it before you make a sale.

Did I overcome objections without encouraging argument?

The Roughneck was the one sales manager who insisted that the words "without an argument" be made a part of Point 13, and said why. "When I began selling," he explained, "I think I got into more arguments with customers than any two salesmen who worked for the company. We had all been trained to handle objections and we'd been told in no uncertain terms that we were to avoid arguments with prospects. Well, I couldn't avoid them. If there'd been a prize for arguments, I'd have won the sweepstakes. I finally got so desperate to solve the problem that I took it to my sales manager. A salesman has to be in real hot water before he'll do a thing like that. Most of my men would step in front of a truck before they'd admit to me that they needed help.

He Was Overdoing Politeness

"I was surprised when I saw that the sales manager was pleased about my coming to him. When I later became a sales manager, I learned that any guy is always tickled pink to have one of his men come to him with a selling problem. It makes him feel that he's earning his salary, and it sorta confirms that he's the expert.

"My sales manager went all out. He told me that he'd go out with me on my next few calls.

"After he'd listened to three arguments with customers, he had my problem in the bag. 'Jim,' he said, 'you're encouraging arguments by trying too hard to avoid them. You're so timid and polite about answering an objection that the customer feels he has you on the run. Instead of giving a yes-but answer, you're giving a definitely-yes-but-don't-you-think-maybe answer. You're so worried about creating antagonism that you're hesitant. The man you're calling on figures you're unsure about your answer. In trying to train you not to have a chip on your shoulder, we've made a Casper Milquetoast out of you. You're not answering the objections with any authority or conviction.'

"On my next call, he took over. We ran into the same objection, and my sales manager gave the man the same answer I'd used. He was pleasant about it, but he was real positive. He made facts sound like facts, and no question about it. Argument just didn't materialize.

147

"It still took me a dozen calls to reach the point where I could follow in his footsteps. I was so afraid of argument that I couldn't believe I could be so positive without getting into a hassle. Once I sold myself that I could do it, the trouble went right down the drain.

"I just wanted to point out that it's possible to encourage argument by not giving a strong enough answer to an objection."

Thank you, Mr. Roughneck. Point noted.

14. Did I do
a positive job of selling,
all the way?

Let's face it, chums—some salesmen sell dirty. They run you down and they lie about you and your product or service. They will even tell derogatory stories about you, if they think you've made a good impression on the prospect.

Yes, they sell dirty—but they don't sell much. They don't sell the same man often—and they're usually replaced in short order when complaints reach their employer.

Even so, there's a lot of selling where the salesman tears his competition to pieces. He's downright vicious.

Nothing on the Record

You almost never see such selling in printed advertising. Why? Because when you put this kind of selling into print or preserve it on TV film or radio tape, its painfully apparent what bad selling it is. A sales manager who is tolerant of this kind of selling by his men in the field would scream to high heaven if the firm's advertising sold the same way. He'd say, "This has to stop. It's making us look bad."

The champion in any sport usually speaks of his challengers with great respect, although he may secretly feel that they're bums. He knows what he's doing. Beating a bum doesn't get him much credit. Beating a man he has touted as great makes him look even greater. No smart football coach ever says to the press, "We're playing a bunch of patsies this year. There isn't a game on our schedule that we shouldn't win by at least three touchdowns." Ever since the days of "Stagg Fears Purdue," coaches of top schools have said that while maybe Upper Iowa didn't get much attention last year in the national ratings, they had a great team and from what information is available, this year's Upper Iowas are even better. They could well be the surprise team of the nation. They have a quarterback who, with a few publicity breaks, could wind up an All-American.

I've known salesmen who, when asked about a competitive product, would become almost violent. They would pay their negative respects to the company, its engineers, its production line, its raw materials, and its finished product.

How much smarter is an RCA distributor salesman. I heard him talking to a dealer who had remarked that a certain competitor had a mighty fine television set.

Making the Competition a Bully

"Yes," Henry agreed, "they certainly have. And they're getting better every year. I think their cabinetry is especially good. Of course, I should say nice things about them because they use some of our basic patents. We really have a rather unfair advantage over them, because we happen to own so many important patents. And we have a rather unfair advantage over them because of the extra time we've been in the color set business. We've naturally led in extra refinements, and nobody's yet close to us in marketing help for our dealers. If we had to start on even terms with them, they might give us fits. They have fine management and a mighty good sales organization. Being a salesman, I sometimes wish their sales staff weren't quite so good. They sometimes overcome advantages of ours that I don't think I could do if I were in their shoes."

When the big boy in any field uses negative selling against his competitors, he creates sympathy for them. He looks like a big, crude bully who's mercilessly trying to crush all competition.

Did I do a positive job of selling, all the way?

And when the little fellow tries to tear down the big boy, more often than not, he simply looks ridiculous. He builds up the old "If you're so smart, why ain't you rich?" feeling in the minds of his customers.

Some years ago, I handled the advertising of a group of dry cleaning establishments that were all owned by one man. He had a virtual monopoly on the cleaning business in his community. If business got slow in the cleaning business, he always started a dry-cleaning price war between his various shops.

Sound Research on Price Cutting

He learned an interesting thing. Invariably, the smallest of his shops got the biggest increase in business while these "wars" were on. Apparently, people felt that the price-cutting was instigated by the big cleaning establishments to try to run the little ones out of business, and they resented it.

At my suggestion, he tried an experiment. Since the price war never got much additional business for his three largest companies, he took this advertising approach with the largest one. "We Are NOT a Part of the Cleaning Price War! We believe in competition. We think it's healthy—and we don't think it's sound for any firm in any kind of business to sell at a loss. We recognize that it's sometimes done to drive competitors out of business. If we chose to enter this cleaning price war, we could outlast any cleaning shop in this state. But we don't think it would be either ethical or good for us, any more than we think it's sensible for smaller companies to get into a price-cutting hassle."

The editorial-type copy continued with a good picture of the quality work turned out by this advertiser. who refused to compromise on his service. You had assurance, the copy said, that any cleaning you sent to this establishment would receive the same careful attention as always, with no temptation to use dirty solvents, to skip over costly hand-spotting of garments, to do machine pressing or take any shortcuts.

And on this particular price war, the big shop, the one with the most business, increased its volume more than the smaller shops did.

Maybe the public doesn't always play fair, but it believes in fair play and respects it.

Sometimes you're in a situation where you simply have to do comparative selling. Let's say a competitor is giving you a rough time on design. You could say, "Their design stinks. It's so bad that I don't see how any intelligent buyer could go for it." Or you could say, "We won three major awards for design this year. These awards are given by design experts who know their stuff. I think our design awards are one reason why our volume is up for this quarter and our competitors' is down. The competitive design you just mentioned is good, though—no question about it. And I'm glad to see such recognition of design's importance to sales. I don't see how improved design can fail to help the entire industry. I hope that competitor and others continue to improve their design."

A certain washing machine manufacturer did a good selling job on the claim that its machine used less water than any other machine ever put on the market. It was a good economy appeal. As it turned out, the appeal was so effective that competition began slugging at it, making remarks that were practically slanderous.

Again, Ask the Man Who Owns One

A salesman in a Chicago appliance store handled it this way. "This water-saving feature must be terrific," he said, "because our competitors are really taking pot-shots at it. You don't knock anything that hard unless it's mighty good. Some of my customers have told me that competitors even say this feature doesn't work satisfactorily. Well, all I know is that we haven't had one solitary complaint. I won't compare the feature to old-fashioned rinsing systems because I don't believe in knocking the other fellow. But if you want the real information on this feature, ask somebody who owns one of our machines rather than a competitor who doesn't happen to have the feature in his machine."

Did I do a positive job of selling, all the way?

That comes close to negative selling without quite getting there—and the curse is taken off the reference to competition.

One manufacturer, faced with untruthful comparisons made by its competitors, hired a testing bureau to make careful tests of all leading makes. Salesmen selling the product were instructed, "Don't get into any fight with competitive makes." Simply say something like this. "Naturally, I'm partial to this particular brand because I sell it. You wouldn't have any more reason to believe what I say about the comparative merits of the various brands of this product than you'd have to believe what our competitors say. I'd suggest that you simply check this product research report made by an independent testing laboratory. Since it covers specific things, and covers them scientifically, you might get a less biased picture than I or any other salesman might give you."

Negative selling? Almost, but not quite. Again, the curse is taken off by a carefully planned approach.

The Curse of Faint Praise

One of the most difficult approaches to use in this area, but an effective one when it's used subtly, is the "damning with faint praise" technique. In a way, it's a continuation of the "Yes, but" approach we discussed under Point 13.

"All things considered," the hi-fi salesman said, "I'd have to say that the CDE set is a good value for the price. It's unfortunate that they felt they had to hold the price a couple of dollars under our economy model. For example, a thing known as an 'L pad' in the speaker system would have made an unbelievable improvement in tonal quality, but it would have cost 67 cents to insert. The engineering in the set is good. If they'd just spent that extra 67 cents, I think they could have given us quite a run for our money."

A sports car salesman said, "They really have a snappy looking model. It handles real well, too. When you stop to figure how little it would have cost to install dual carburetors at the factory, you could cry. We know how much increase in efficiency dual carburetors mean to *our* car, and I think it would mean just as much to theirs."

In both of these instances, comparative selling was necessary, because of what competitors were doing. The hi-fi competitor was saying, "Our set is priced lower than theirs and the quality is better." Actually, the elimination of the L pad did hurt tonal quality and was a manufacturing error.

The sports-car salesman's competitor was saying, "They try to make a big deal out of dual carburetors and they sock you plenty for them. We'd rather save you the money."

The Old Timer said, "When I began selling, practically everybody in the line I was in sold dirty. Our sales manager had dug up all the dirt in our competitors' past and told us not only to use it but to hit hard. I suspect that some of the ammunition he gave us was gross exaggeration, if not complete untruth. The excuse for getting into the mud was that 'you had to fight fire with fire.'

"That kind of selling didn't appeal to me and I ignored my sales manager's instructions. I told myself that I was too busy selling our line to spend time knocking the other fellow's.

"We were in a special field where a salesman had to be almost an engineer. Training a new man took time. Well, our company merged with a competitor—actually was taken over by the competitor. The sales force in the other company stayed, and our men were out.

The Word Got Back

"We didn't worry much about it, because we knew that good men in this particular field were darned hard to find. I got a job with a bigger company, almost immediately, without much discussion.

"A couple of months later, I saw Roger Ess, one of the top salesmen with the old company, in a coffee shop. He came over and sat beside me. 'How in blazes did you ever manage to get a job?' he asked. 'Do you realize that you're the only guy in the whole crew who's been able to land anything?' I asked Roger what the problem was, and he

154

Did I do a positive job of selling, all the way?

said, 'They all tell me they'd like to hire me but that it wouldn't work because I've told all my customers what an awful product they had and what a horrible company they operated. They said it just wouldn't make sense to prospective buyers for me to be selling for them.'

"I went back and talked to my new sales manager and he confirmed what Roger had told me. 'To be honest,' he said, 'I'd have liked to hire five of your old company's men. Unfortunately, you were the only one of the five I dared to put on. The others had all sold hard on what a bad setup we had. For them to suddenly walk in and sing our praises wouldn't have made sense.'

It's Self-Protection

"I think the point I'm trying to make is that you not only add to the stature of your company but you protect yourself when you don't knock your competitor. I wasn't thinking of that when I ignored instructions to smear the other companies—but my decision certainly worked out to my advantage. I've been selling for a good many years, and I've never asked a salesman to knock a competitor. I've never had any reason to regret that attitude. I probably have more stature in the business than I deserve. Part of it is due to the number of years I've been around—but I think more of it can be credited to my never having earned the enmity of anybody else in the field. Nobody can say that I've ever played dirty.

"Then how do I feel about the competitors who have taken business away from me by dirty tactics? I feel darned sorry for them. For every dollar's worth of business they've gotten that way, I've eventually wound up with five when customers thought things out.

"Another thing, the best salesmen with our competitors have picked our company as their goal, because they know we won't get into mud-slinging contests. They reason that we must be the best.

"What's more, we *are* the best, if for no other reason than our refusal to rap competition."

The customer sometimes deliberately tries to get you into a negative selling position. He gets a kick out of hearing two competing salesmen

155

tear each other to pieces. But remember that tearing each other to pieces is exactly what they do. Nobody wins. I once told the sales manager of a network of a charge that a rival network sales manager had made against him, and his only comment was the old, old one, "I never get into an acid-throwing contest with a skunk."

I've never known a salesman who got drawn into a knocking contest who didn't regret it. Remember, you're a pro—and a pro is too good to need to knock.

In the town in Nebraska where I ran a community weekly newspaper, two candidates for county office got into a mean, personal campaign. It was finally arranged for them to meet in a public debate, in which accusations flew all over the place. They did everything short of questioning each other's ancestry.

As I was leaving the debate, I heard one Nebraska farmer ask another one, "Well, what do you think?" And the other one replied, "Damned if I haven't reached the conclusion that they're both a hundred percent right."

The old "Every knock is a boost" saw is much too much of a generality. I've heard knocks that were anything but boosts. But I *will* buy this: Every knock is a sign of fear or respect or both.

Some Hypothetical Questions

As an exercise, let's assume that you are selling Flamingo automobiles. A competitive salesman, selling Pelican cars, is telling all prospects that the brakes on the Flamingo are dangerously unsafe. Actually, the Flamingo brakes are superior to the Pelican's. How would you handle the situation?

Now, let's say that a Flamingo owner is killed in a car crash. The Pelican competitor spreads a story that the man's death was due to faulty brakes, despite any comparative brake ratings you have. How would you handle this?

Let's take another situation. You are selling insurance, and a competing salesman spreads the story that your company is notori-

Did I do a positive job of selling, all the way?

ously slow in settling claims. The fact is that your company *is* slightly slower than his, because your company makes a careful investigation of every claim before payment. How would you handle the competitor's story?

X brand television sets are outselling your Y brand. You know for a fact that X brand has gone to an inferior picture tube with a much shorter life expectancy than the tube in Y sets. How can you handle a good selling point for yourself without seeming to knock a competitor? What do you say without damaging the character of your company's business conduct?

A competitor is telling his prospects that you're involved in a marital scandal, which is untrue. Several customers tell you about it. What do you do?

How would you handle the statement by a competing salesman that your product or service is grossly overpriced?

15. Did I avoid
letting the customer get me off
the main sales line?

As an advertising man with Ruthrauff & Ryan advertising agency, I called on an account with the express idea of selling $200,000 worth of local television spot advertising. It was an extremely difficult account to handle, seldom staying with any campaign or project long enough to get it established.

This was a sale I really wanted to make, because it was not only right for the customer but had to be bought under such a firm contract that the usual hopping in and out couldn't be done. It was a deal that would protect the client from himself, for once.

The presentation was painstakingly prepared. I hadn't assumed that the prospect knew *anything* about the proposal. I had proof points galore, all carefully translated into benefits.

Boat Enters Conversation

I knew almost everything there was to know about this particular prospect, having cultivated him for months. We were on the best of terms, personally. And I knew that the man respected my ability and judgment, at least as much as he respected anybody's.

The solicitation started beautifully. I didn't get "Yesses" from him, which I hadn't expected, because nobody ever did—but I was at least getting "Well, maybe," and "Possibly," and "Uh, yes and no. Maybe you're right." These remarks from this client were so unusual that I felt the order was in my pocket.

Did I avoid getting off the main sales line?

I was just leading into good old Point 10 and it was a killer, when the client smiled at me.

"George," he interrupted what I was saying, "did I ever show you any pictures of my boat?"

It was startling, not to say unnerving. "What?" I asked.

"Did I ever show you any pictures of my boat?" he repeated. "I know you're interested in boats, and I have some pictures that are real beauties."

Fifty Minutes Down the Drain

He opened a drawer in his rolltop desk and, so help me, he pulled out a pile of glossy prints a foot high. There were pictures of that cabin cruiser in dry dock, on a trailer truck, in inland lakes, in Florida waters—pictures from every conceivable angle. Most of the pictures had people in them, and he felt it his duty to explain to me who they were.

He talked about those pictures and that boat for 50 uninterrupted minutes. I know exactly how long he talked, because I timed it. And then he wanted my reactions. Did I think the boat was too big for him? How did I feel about metal, fiberglass, and mahogany hulls? Was his motor big enough, in my opinion? Or was it too big?

I tried to get back to the solicitation. Believe me, I tried. But just as I was about to make it, he looked at his watch and announced that it was time for lunch—and it was.

I tried to get back onto the subject of television spots during lunch, but he still wanted to talk about his boat. He was determined to talk about it. He did talk about it.

By the time we got back to his office, that presentation was deader than the proverbial mackerel, and I was trying desperately to keep my anger from showing through. He finally mentioned that he had just put the boat into the water.

"Say," I said, "I have a great idea. I've never been on your boat. I know you don't ordinarily go out during working hours, but let's kill two birds with one stone. I'll have to start this material from the beginning again, anyway—so why don't we go aboard and I'll do the presentation there?"

He beamed "Nobody could say I was goofing off," he nodded. "Let's go."

There's nothing I'd like better than to be able to tell you that I made the sale on the boat—but I didn't. Once aboard, he insisted on showing me every detail. He threw the whole presentation out again with conversation about the boat. I not only didn't close the sale but I didn't come within a country mile of closing it.

Afterward, asking myself the question, "Did I avoid letting the customer get me off the main sales line?" I had to answer, "I sure as blazes didn't."

And I knew what I should have done but hadn't done. I knew in advance how limited this man's span of attention was and how difficult it was for him to make a decision under the most favorable circumstances. Knowing these things, when he asked me if I'd seen pictures of his boat, I should have said, "No, and I'd love to see them as soon as I get through going over this material. We're so deeply into it now that I'm afraid I'd have difficulty getting back on the track if I were to stop."

A Direct Protest Worked

Would this have offended him? Possibly. If it would have, I certainly wouldn't have been any worse off than I was. I'd have come much closer to making a sale, offended or not.

There was another time when I was trying to sell an advertising service to a newspaper advertising director who kept taking phone calls during the first five minutes of my presentation. It was my first call on the man.

Did I avoid getting off the main sales line?

"Mister Zee," I said after his third phone call, "I don't think you're being fair to me."

"Whadda yah mean?" he growled.

"You need an advertising service," I said, "and I came all the way out from Chicago to show you this one and explain it to you in detail. If you know anything I've said up to this point, you're way ahead of me. I don't. Is there anywhere we could go where we might get a half hour to concentrate on this?"

"We can do it right here," he said, and called for his secretary. "No phone calls and no interruptions for the next half hour," he told her.

Most Delays Unintentional

When the presentation was over and he had signed a year's contract, he said, "Young man, that was a clever trick you used."

"Trick?" I asked.

"Accusing me of being unfair to you. You put me in a position where I was determined to prove to you that I would give you a fair hearing. You put me right square on defense. I knew when I told the girl to hold up my calls that I was going to buy your ad service."

I hadn't thought of it that way, but I was grateful for the order. You know, it really *might* be a good trick with some prospects under some circumstances.

It's been my experience that most of the customers who try to pull you off the main sales line don't do it intentionally. They don't do it to annoy you or to discourage you. A good many of them don't even realize that they're doing it.

The most difficult man to handle on this point is one like the fellow with the boat, a man whose attention span is too brief. If his mind habitually wanders under any circumstances, it shouldn't be surprising that it wanders during your solicitation.

This type of buyer is difficult to sell even if he *doesn't* get you off the line. Let's face it, if your solicitation is any good, it's always easier to sell a bright man than a slow one. He concentrates, he asks intelligent questions and he knows when you've made a point. He doesn't want to waste time any more than you do.

But let's face another thing. If you make many calls, you'll run into a few prospects who range from slightly slow to plain moronic.

Keeping them on the track is always a problem—and it's a problem for the best pro who ever made a sale.

When I run across one of these wandering minds, I don't get mad at anyone except myself—and what I get mad at myself about is that a dope of this caliber is able to get me sidetracked.

Maybe my way of handling this situation would be frowned on by some sales managers, but it works for me.

If a man is wandering from the sales message, I immediately jazz up the presentation. On occasion, I've made it practically a one-man vaudeville show. Instead of using research to prove a point, I may do it with a joke—and not a very subtle joke. The demonstration may include a little magic. I hadn't realized it, but an associate says that in a situation like this, I talk louder and faster than I normally do. I bear down harder, and instead of trying to get the prospect to talk at length, I try to get him to say "Yes." I try to give him as little chance as I can to say any more than that by the time we're reaching the summary.

Head for the Summary

The Personality Kid says he heads for a summary as fast as he can when anyone tries to get him off the track. But he *drives* home the facts of his summary. He makes it almost a capsule sales solicitation.

How you handle the wandering mind is going to depend on your personality—but it's something you should work out carefully, even if by trial and error—because you must handle it, one way or another.

Did I avoid getting off the main sales line?

The way the bright prospect most often gets you off the main sales line is by belaboring one minor point in your solicitation. You haven't sold him on it and he isn't going to let go. If you let yourself get into an involved discussion, it can sometimes last for hours that you can't spare.

The Scientist says, "This gets back to answering objections, and the way I handle it isn't the perfect way. I use the 'Yes, but' technique. I concede that he may have a point and get onto a counterbalancing point as quickly as I can. A smart buyer feels that I've been fair with him and that he should be equally fair with me on the counterbalancing point."

"Dear Sir: You May Be Right. Sincerely,"

The late H. L. Mencken in his prime tried to answer all his personal mail—and a lot of it came from indignant crackpots who thought he should be boiled in oil. He handled this lunatic fringe mail perfectly. Regardless of how preposterous any letter was, Mencken answered it, "Dear Mr. So-and-so: You may be right. Sincerely, H. L. Mencken." There are times when you must do almost the same thing to avoid being pulled far afield.

One salesman told me about a customer who simply wouldn't let him stick to his solicitation. "All he wanted to talk about," this fellow said, "was a grievance he had against the company."

That's not unique—but a man like this doesn't pull you *off* the main sales line. He won't let you get *on* it. You have to discuss that grievance and try to take care of it before you even *begin* your sales presentation. Once you've listened to the complaint and promised to see what can be done about it, this man will usually give you his undivided attention. He's made his point.

A man who sells work clothes told me about being pulled off the sales line by a customer who was usually attentive and cooperative. On this particular day, however, he had a one-track mind. He wanted to know why the company didn't add tan work shirts to their line.

"No matter what I tried to talk about," the salesman said, "this kook kept talking about tan work shirts. He had the names of retail customers who wanted tan work shirts. He had story after story about how he lost sales by not having them in stock. He had three or four theories about why people wanted tan work shirts. I told him at least five times that I'd see what I could do about it—and that turned out to be a mistake, because then he wanted to give me all his ammunition to use with the company.

"He talked about tan work shirts until I was ready to scream for help. My call was almost a total loss. I sold him less than I'd ever sold him. I was disgusted enough so that I passed on everything he's said.

"The sales manager told me I should have been able to talk him out of it. 'You try talking him out of it,' I said. And darned if he didn't go out and call on the guy. Know what happened? The two of them worked out a line of tan work shirts. And wanta know something else? They sell! They're a strong addition to the line."

There are temptations to leave the sales track almost every time you make a solicitation—but if you're well prepared, temptations won't bother you. You'll hew to the line. The trouble is almost never temptations—it's road blocks. The customer *demands* that you talk about something irrelevant.

Watch For "Detour" Signs

On this point, the advertising copywriter's job is a breeze compared to the salesman's. The copywriter writes his ad copy right straight through to the finish. Nobody interrupts him and nobody throws curves at him while he's making his printed offer.

Of course, he doesn't have much way of knowing whether he held the reader's attention all the way through or not. And the salesman always knows.

Being aware that detour signs during some of your presentations are almost inevitable, it becomes increasingly important to know

Did I avoid getting off the main sales line?

where you're going before you start. The poorly prepared salesman gets sidetracked far more often than the one who plans.

If you do let the customer get you off the main line, it's vital to ask yourself, "Why did he do it?" Weren't you getting through to him? Had you lost his viewpoint? Weren't you talking his language? Was the part of your presentation where the detour occurred dull and uninteresting? Should you have gone directly into a hard-hitting summary?

Some Detective Work

A fellow who sells automobiles made an interesting discovery on Point 15. He suddenly realized, while we were discussing it, that he was getting sidetracked on every sales solicitation, always at the same point. When he began his sales talk on "Wide Track," which was a feature of the car, he began getting questions and remarks that had nothing to do with what he was talking about.

He gave that part of his solicitation to me, just as he'd been doing it. And I'll have to admit that all it did was confuse me. I had thought I knew about wide track, but by the time he got through, I was in a fog.

If your presentation doesn't seem to be making sense at a certain point, you can't blame the prospect for wanting to talk about something else—something he understands.

There is always a simple way to explain anything—at least a way that doesn't create added confusion.

Are you being lured from the sales line at a certain point in your presentation? If sidetracks come at specific places, you know there has to be something wrong at those points.

A friend of mine told me that he had what he thought was a carefully planned solicitation, with everything well worked out. And yet, he said, he had bad trouble with Point 15. He asked if I'd listen to his presentation, and I was glad to do it.

165

I should say, I was glad to do it for the first hour. His solicitation made sense every step of the way—but what a way. It was so interminably long that you could hardly expect any prospect to sit through it. Few men's bladders would hold out that long, let alone their minds.

Another salesman who had trouble with Point 15 was selling food freezers. He was a conscientious fellow, and he thought the sales manual was so excellent that he incorporated the whole thing into his sales solicitation. It was a fine sales manual, loaded with information that the salesman should have had, in case he needed it on occasion. But nobody had ever intended for any prospect to sit through the entire book. Few prospects did, as this salesman learned.

An insurance salesman who had read extensively about making friends prided himself on learning everything there was to know about each prospect. Then he interlarded everything he said with little personal remarks, so much so that all the way through, he practically invited discussions about things that had nothing to do with the prospect's need for insurance. He made a bad thing of a good thing by overdoing it.

Humor certainly has its place in selling, and I've always used it. But telling too many jokes can be fatal. There are prospects who pride themselves on the many funny stories that *they know*, and if you aren't careful, you can get yourself into a joke-swapping session that the prospect thoroughly enjoys, that can go on for hours, but, unfortunately, doesn't stay on the track that leads to a sale.

A Self-Test on Point 15

To prompt your thinking about Point 15:

1. What dangerous remarks can you think of that might invite the customer to lead you off the main sales line?

2. You're trying to sell a set of reference books to a woman, and she interrupts to give you a new recipe that she's sure your wife will like. Your sales solicitation is reaching a climax. How do you handle it?

Did I avoid getting off the main sales line?

3. You're selling the economy benefit, which reminds the customer of a tightwad friend of his. It's obvious that he has a fund of stories about the man. What do you do?

4. If a non sequitur interruption comes during your presentation of your product's exclusive advantage, what does it indicate to you?

16. Did I encourage the customer to ask questions, and did I answer them intelligently?

Right at the outset of your sales solicitation, in the Personal Points, we had Point 4, "Did I encourage the customer to do part of the talking?" This began to get the customer involved, and it helped you to learn the basic desire or need of his so that you could capitalize on it (Point 3).

Later on, in the Proof Points, we came to Point 9, "Did I make the customer participate in the demonstration?" This created an even further involvement on his part.

Now, at Point 16, we're getting near the close—and we want still more customer participation. You've already had customer objections and have answered them. You've handled the opposition positively, without openly knocking a competitive product or service. You've stayed right on the main sales line and you're really rolling, drawing closer and closer to a sale.

Clearing Track For Close

At this time, you ask the customer, "Do you have any further questions? Are there any points about owning this that aren't quite clear to you?"

You're getting that track completely cleared, so that the home stretch is wide open, without a barrier.

Did I encourage questions, and answer them intelligently?

If at this point, the customer brings up an objection he's previously made, you can be dead sure that your way of answering it didn't convince him. Maybe you should now take a different approach to overcoming the objection. If you used "Yes, but," maybe at this point you should go into a number of counterbalancing benefits. Maybe you didn't completely answer his previous objection because you didn't quite understand it.

At this juncture, he's giving you another chance—so don't muff it.

Quite often, in your invitation for questions, you'll get the tip that you're at the point of a sale. "What kind of financing arrangements can I make?" or "How soon can you guarantee delivery?" are welcome words to any salesman's ear. So are questions about cash discounts.

Light at Tunnel's End

Whatever questions you get this time around should be indicator dials to show where you stand.

A real estate saleswoman, selling a house in the $60,000 range, told me about a case where the question at this point was, "Does this development have any restrictive covenants?"

"Absolutely none," she replied.

"Then," the man answered, "I'm not interested. I want some controls over who my neighbors are going to be. I've looked at two other houses that aren't quite as nice as this one, but they have good, strong restrictive covenants. After all, I should have the right to live in an area where I'll find the kind of people I want to associate with."

"So you lost the sale?" I asked.

"No," she said. "I *made* the sale by admitting that I didn't know the answer about restrictive clauses. I said to him, 'Before you buy any property on the strength of a restrictive clause, ask your lawyer if it will stand up in court.' He called his lawyer, right then and there. The lawyer told him that the restrictive clauses in the titles of the two houses he'd looked at weren't worth the paper they were printed on and could actually cause trouble for him. So I went real fast into a summary of the features of the house I was showing, inviting a comparison with the other two houses. He bought."

Sometimes the only questions you get at this stage of the solicitation will signal you to skip the summary and get to the close as quickly as you can.

But sometimes, as in the case of the man buying the house, you get a question that seems to come right out of left field, something that hasn't come up at all and which looks like it could be a real stopper.

One time I was selling a costly television campaign to the advertising manager of an important company. Everything had gone beautifully. The opposition questions had been answered to the fellow's satisfaction, and he suggested that we continue the discussion over lunch. We went to lunch and everything continued to go smoothly until I asked him if he had any further questions.

"Just one," he said, looking me right in the eye. "Can I get a new Cadillac out of this sale?"

I pretended not to know what he was talking about. "The program should certainly help to establish your value to the company," I answered. "I've no way of knowing, but I'd say it's entirely possible you could get a nice raise on the strength of such a buy."

"I'll take care of the company," he said. "What I want to know is what I can get from you?"

Free Cadillac Too Expensive

"Not one damn thing," I told him. "In the first place, we don't do business that way. I know there are firms that do, but if you had wanted to do business with them, you'd have gone to them first. In the second place, getting a free Cadillac would be too expensive for you. I'd make too much on it."

"Just what do you mean by that?" he demanded.

"Nobody gives away $6,000 of his profit on a deal, ever," I explained. "Once you took the Cadillac, my company would have you

Did I encourage questions, and answer them intelligently?

right over a barrel. We could cut corners in every direction. We could cut quality to an absolute minimum—and you wouldn't dare protest. As a matter of fact, you'd have to defend us to your company. You wouldn't be working for them; you'd have to work for us, whether you liked it or not.

"Anyway," I said, "I know that you didn't mean it when you asked if you could get a new Cadillac. You didn't know whether my company was honest or not and you were just probing to find out. Well, you have your answer."

"I'm glad you realize what I was doing," he said, weakly. "Of course, if you had offered to *give* me the Cadillac, the whole deal would have been off."

Stay Out of Traps

Of course. Sure, it would.

"I know," I nodded. "You have much too important and too good a job to risk your whole business life on a free automobile. You're too smart to even think about such a thing seriously. Do you have any other questions?"

"How far ahead would we have to work on commercials?"

I told him, and then asked for the order, without ever going into the summary. And a sale was closed.

You can't anticipate questions like that one. And sometimes, you have to do some mighty fast ad-libbing. You'll notice that Point 16 says, "did I answer the questions intelligently?"

Intelligently is the key word. I don't believe for one minute that the advertising manager I just mentioned was probing. I think he was asking for a kickback. But quite often at this point in the sales presentation you'll get trick questions, queries designed to trap you in one way or another.

And sometimes the only intelligent answer you can give is "I don't know, but I'll try to find out for you." If ever there was a wrong point at which to bluff, this is it.

You increase your stature with the prospective customer when you admit you can't answer a question and go to the phone to try to get the correct answer. He immediately gets the idea that he's dealing with a man who's careful of what he says, who isn't going to give him a con job.

"Intelligently" also means "truthfully." It's never bright to lie about anything involved in a sale.

I had a salesman working for me one time who was a chronic liar. Many times when the truth would have been simpler and more effective, he lied. And I simply couldn't show him the error of his ways.

In the process of making a sales solicitation, he would think of some fanciful story that at the moment seemed more effective than the true story he'd been given. It was often enough so ridiculous that he lost the sale. And when he did make a sale, there were repercussions and adjustments.

One time, he made unauthorized promises on which he couldn't possibly deliver, and I made him go back to the customer and admit to him that he's been overenthusiastic and so eager to make the sale that he'd stretched the truth.

The answer he got from the customer, a "borax" merchant, didn't come under the reading of helpful things to say to teach the young man to straighten up and fly right.

The Elastic Conscience

"Young fella," the merchant said to him, "I hope this teaches you a lesson that I learned years ago. Never lie in business unless you know that you're completely covered from every angle."

Well, I guess it takes one to know one.

When you get this far along in a sale and still don't know where you stand, there is a horrible temptation to stretch the truth.

Did I encourage questions, and answer them intelligently?

I was all set to give a highly colored answer once, and something stopped me just in time. My answer was, "I'd like to tell you so-and-so in answer to your questions—and I think I might be fairly close to right—but there's no way I could possibly prove it."

"I was trying to trap you," the prospect grinned. "I've already talked to your boss about this and have the right answer. Both of your competitors gave me the answer that you didn't quite give me— the one all three of you knew I'd like to hear. Where's the order blank?"

A Test Question

A friend of mine told me that he'd had a bad week and was really bearing down on a prospect. When he came to the "Any questions?" part of his presentation, he said the fellow stopped him cold.

"Yeah," the prospect said. "I'm just a little guy and you work for a big company. Why are you making such a big deal out of selling me?"

"Because," my friend said, after stopping to think, "I make my living out of getting new customers and keeping them. You're a new customer. If I sell you and keep you happy, it will show up on my record—and my sales record is what gets the baby new shoes. Any more questions?"

The fellow laughed. "Nope," he said. "I ask that question of every new salesman who calls on me. And do you know how most of them answer it? They tell me they wanta help me. Yeah—some of them would help me right out of business. You leveled with me—and people who level with me are the only ones I like to deal with."

No salesman likes to hear one question that sometimes comes at Point 16. "Couldn't you cut the price a little?"

One of the best answers I ever heard to this irksome question came from, of all people, a commercial illustrator.

A newspaper was publishing a 100th anniversary edition and wanted illustrative cover pages for 12 sections of the paper. The advertising director of the paper had good taste and appreciated quality. He was also a born chiseler. He asked me to submit an artist for the job, along with samples of his work. I did. He called and asked me if I could bring the artist out to talk to him. I said I could, knowing what he was planning. He knew that he couldn't chisel me, but he thought the artist would be a pushover.

"Ben," I told the artist, "I want one thing completely understood. If you cut your price one dime, I won't ever submit any of your work to anybody, any place, any time."

"Gotcha," Ben nodded.

Carl, the advertising manager, greeted us effusively. He jut us in deep, comfortable chairs, facing a bright light, and had his boy pour drinks for us.

"Now, let me see," he said, "I'm not sure I remember. What was your price for these pages?"

"Five hundred dollars," Ben answered.

"Five hundred dollars for 12 pages? That seems fair enough."

"No," Ben said. "Five hundred dollars per page. Six thousand dollars for the 12 pages."

The Bargaining Gets Brisk

"Young man," Carl said, "I have to tell you this. I've talked to two artists today who will be happy to take this assignment at less than a hundred dollars a page."

"Oh, I don't doubt that at all," Ben answered. "I can remember when I'd have been glad to do them for 50 bucks apiece."

That stopped Carl momentarily. "I don't mind telling you," he said, "that there's a quality in your work I like. But I'm throttled with budgets. Could you possibly cut that price to, say, $200 per page?"

Did I encourage questions, and answer them intelligently?

"Oh, sure," Ben said. And I withered.

"You mean, you'll do the 12 cover pages for me for $2,400?"

"That's right," Ben agreed. "But I'd slap them out. And if one of them happened to turn out good by accident, as sometimes happens, I'd deliberately louse it up before I delivered it to you."

"Three hundred dollars a page," Carl said.

"I only know how to do two kinds of art work," Ben said. "My best, and deliberately bad. My price for my best is $500 a page. Pay me $495 and you'll get deliberately bad work."

"Well," Carl sighed. "I'll have to talk to the publisher and he isn't around this evening. I'll call you in the morning."

He called Ben at 10 a.m. the next day and I was on a telephone extension.

The Arm-Twisting Continues

"I just got through talking to the publisher," he said, "and after quite a battle, I got him to agree to spend $4,800 for the cover pages. Four hundred dollars apiece."

"Did you explain the situation to him?" Ben asked.

"What do you mean?"

"Well, I think he's awfully foolish to spend $400 apiece for cover pages that will be deliberately bad art work."

"What?"

"I explained my position to you last night. Five hundred dollars per page for my best work. Anything less than that—bad work."

There was a long pause. "All right," Carl said. "Five hundred dollars per page. You have a deal."

The conclusion to the story was most interesting. When Ben delivered the pages, Carl shook hands with him and said, "Ben, they're absolutely beautiful. You're not only a superb artist, but you're a damned fine business man."

Don't blame a chiseler for trying. Carl was a chiseler only because he'd found that he could get away with it a good deal of the time.

And remember this. Once you let a customer chisel you, he has you on the hook for all time. You've proved that you can be whittled down. He never knows how *far* down you'll go, so he keeps trying to find a new bottom point.

And who does the chiseler respect? The man who gives him the lowest price? Not at all. He respects the salesman who won't cut his price one thin dime.

Particularly in the case of services, price cutting is fatal. A service is worth what you can get for it, no more. Once you cut price, that's all it's worth. The word gets around. A chiseler always brags about how much better buys he's made than those around him. Those who paid the fair price are outraged—and rightly so.

Point 16 is hard to prepare for. Oh, there are certain questions that pop up more than others, but this is a part of the solicitation where the salesman must be on his toes, thinking every minute. You must not be thrown by a question that's never been tossed at you before.

This is a point where your ability to maintain your poise and think on your feet sets you far above the amateurs who so often lose sales by panicking.

Ad-Libs Can't Be Taught

One of the sales managers who worked on the 20 Points says, "Point 16 is the one that proves that a good ad-lib can often do more to close a sale than everything that's been carefully planned. I think I'm good at it, and I think being good at it has put me where I am."

"How," one of the other sales managers asked, "do you teach it to your men?"

Did I encourage questions, and answer them intelligently?

"Teach it, hell," the first one said. "Nobody teaches it. You learn it by experience. Either you learn it or you're not one of those absolutely super salesmen."

"But," the scientific sales manager protested, "couldn't we put together every question that's likely to be asked and figure out the best answers for them?"

"Last week," the tough guy who started it all said, "I asked a sales manager, 'Any other questions'? and he said, 'Yeah. Before you get away, my wife is having an affair with the president of the company. How should I handle it?' "

You know, that question probably wouldn't turn up on *any* list.

The Closing of a Sale

More nonsense has been written about the close than about any other part of selling. Of course, there's a perfectly good reason for this. A great many so-called sales "experts" don't really understand the close, so they try to surround it with mysticism. Listening to them, you'd believe that a sudden psychic flash occurs when the proper closing time arrives.

And the close is no place for guesswork. It is obviously the most important part of your entire solicitation, the goal of all your effort.

Good salesmen have told me, "I never had the faintest idea of how to close or when to do it until I ran across and learned Point 19.

A district sales manager for the Staley Company once said in a meeting in New York, "I've been coming to these sales meetings for a good many years, and today I've learned things I wouldn't trade for $15,000. This is the first time in my life I've ever really caught the basic idea of how and when to close a sale."

The highest compliment that his fellow workers can pay a salesman is to say, "He's a great closer."

There are otherwise good salesmen who don't even *try* to close. Rather, they hint at it, skirt around it, and hope that the prospect will ask to buy.

I once worked with a man who had wonderful business contacts. Once he got an appointment, he could charm the prospective customer. He knew sales approaches that were brilliant, and he could come up with just the right benefits to make a specific customer want what he was selling.

He had just one problem. He would not ask for the order. He was actually embarrassed with the idea of asking the prospect to buy. The prospects thought he was a great guy, and a good many of them bought from him because they were so fond of him. (Remember— other things being equal, people buy from people they like.) But *more* prospects *didn't* buy from him for the simple reason that he never asked them for their business. He had the kind of psychological block that no salesman can afford.

Because our boss knew his weakness, he sent me with him on an important solicitation with the instructions, "You hold back and don't say a word until it's time to close. Then move in and take it away from him."

"Wouldn't it be better if I took part all the way along?" I asked.

"No," the boss replied. "I know your failing, too. You're so eager to close, right from the start, that you scare the customer. Let Lou do the selling job just as he always does, and then take over."

It was an 11 o'clock appointment, to be followed by lunch. At 12 o'clock, when we went to eat, it seemed to me that we were all set to get the man's order, but Lou told the prospect there were a few more points he wanted to discuss.

"Why Are We All Here?"

He discussed these over lunch—delightfully. The prospect was enjoying himself thoroughly. So was Lou. Finally, lunch was finished. The prospect stuck his hand across the table and said, "Lou, I can't remember when I've enjoyed a business lunch this much. We'll have to get together again."

I said, "Mr. Jay, you realize why we're here, don't you?" He looked at me with a puzzled little frown on his forehead. Lou looked as if he were going to sink through his chair to the floor.

"Why, it's been most pleasant," Mr. Jay said.

"I think so, too, and I'm glad it *has* been so pleasant, because that should put you in a good mood to sign the order. The reason we're here, you know, is to make a sale."

Lou was mortified at my crude approach. He actually blushed.

"Yeah, I guess you're right," Mr. Jay said. "Do you have an order blank handy?" I did, and he signed it.

I had been prepared to really bear down hard to close that sale, but I didn't need to do anything—anything except ask for the order. If I hadn't asked, the company would have eventually had some business from the man—but not that day or that week.

Being afraid to ask for the order is a more common failing than you might imagine. It's particularly evident with salesmen who aren't sure of themselves, who don't really know whether they're doing a good selling job or not.

There should be no stigma attached to asking for the order. You aren't begging for business. You've shown the prospect that he should have what you're selling. You're in business to make sales, and you've earned this one. He knows that you didn't call on him simply to bask in his charm. He's fully aware that you came in quest of business. That's your livelihood. He expects you to ask for the order, whether he gives it to you or not.

Got Order on Tenth Try

And a good salesman doesn't turn tail and run at the first "No." I saw one of my salesmen at the Chicago *Tribune* Newspaper Advertising Service ask point-blank for the order 10 times—and get it on the 10th try.

Just as a good ad extends an invitation to buy, so does a good salesman. Asking for the order makes it easier for the prospect to buy. Making that decision alone, without a prompter from you, is difficult for many customers. They want you to push them into a decision.

180

There are a few executives who simply can't make decisions by themselves. They're either scared to death of making a wrong decision or they don't want to ripple the waves by making *any* decision. I worked once for a man who absolutely would not say "Yes" or "No." He boasted that he hadn't made a mistake in 10 years. Of course, he hadn't. He hadn't really *done* anything in 10 years.

People who worked under him had to, in desperation, make the decisions he should have made. His usual charming comment was, "Well, you better be right."

When you are selling a man like this, you don't need to feel the slightest embarrassment at being persistent. You must stay in there and pound a decision out of him. And maybe it's odd, but this type of man is almost never annoyed at your persistence. I guess he feels in his mind that he's forcing you to make the decision for him.

Hang in There and Ask

Over the years, I've seen many salesmen make the close more difficult than it really is. They rightly attach much importance to it, but they let that importance throw them.

The Roughneck says, "I preach asking for the order to all my men. I tell them it's the most important single thing they can do. But I'll bet you that nearly 50% of my men's calls are completed without a real do-or-die try at closing. I don't really like brashness in a young man, but I hire the brash boys because I know they'll have the guts to ask for the order and keep on asking."

In radio, we used to "tag" dramatic scenes with music. At the end of a scene, there was a musical "stinger" that said, in effect, "This scene is finished." At the end of each act and at the end of the drama, there was "big" music that told the audience it was over. You wouldn't have dreamed of leaving out those musical indicators. Well, the close is the end of the sales solicitation, a needed conclusion. You "wrap things up" with an order or a turndown—and you can't get either without inviting—even demanding—it.

There are some important things to know about the close that may help overcome any fears of it.

1. The customer expects it. He knows you're there to sell him something. If you leave without asking for the order, he has to feel let down. He wasted his time.

2. He wants you to ask for the order. Except in wildly ideal situations, he doesn't want to volunteer it. He wants you to try to close, and this is true whether he's made up his mind to buy or not.

3. He rarely gets mad at persistence, even if you ask for the order a number of times. People respect competence in any field, and your customer knows that a good salesman tries hard for the order.

4. If you fail to ask for the order a few times when you think it wouldn't do any good, you start to acquire a terribly bad habit.

5. You rob your company when you fail to ask for the order. Think of what a sales call costs your employer. You may not make the sale, but you can at least earn your money by trying.

6. You have no right to fail to close, because closing is an integral part of selling. If you wanted to keep a room warm, you wouldn't lay a fire and then fail to apply a match to it. It is stupid to make a solicitation and then not ask for the order.

Mail-order advertising is the most checkable advertising there is. I've never seen a mail-order ad that didn't ask for the order. In many mail-order ads, there's even a coupon, where all you have to do is sign your name and address. Mail-order advertisers know that the way to get money coming in is to ask for it.

Face this fact. If you're going to be a seller, you have to be a closer.

17. Did I give the customer logical reasons why he would benefit from immediate purchase?

It's easier to put off buying than it is to buy right now. "I'm pretty sure I'm going to buy your product, but I'd like to think it over for a few days" has been the end of many a sale.

In my early days of selling, I remember many cases where I had the sale "in the bag"—oh, you could definitely count on it, but it was going to take a few days. Those sales were in the bag, all right, but somebody usually ripped open the bottom of the bag.

If you want to close a sale without a call-back—and of course you do—you need at least one good reason for immediate purchase—a reason for not putting off 'til tomorrow what you want that customer to do right now.

There are always reasons for immediate purchase, some much more convincing than others. The easiest to work with, in my experience, are the Special Inducements.

"Special Low Price for a Limited Time Only." "Extra Added Offer This Week Only." "Sale Price While Limited Supply Lasts." "Free— A Beautiful New Whatchamacallit with Every Purchase Made Now." "Today Only—Special Trial Offer." "Final Closeout at This Low Price." "Never Again a Price Cut Like This."

My old friend, Bob Kahn, a master at mail-order selling, once told me that if you really wanted an item to move, you offered something free with it "for immediate orders."

In the advertising agency business, I've seen manufacturers testing a new product in department stores who disdained the "Special Inducement." And they've fallen right on their faces. To get action on a new item, you need a spur.

To get orders on *anything,* you need a spur, too.

I know one salesman whose company has a generous cooperative advertising program for retailers. A certain size purchase gets a certain amount of advertising money. Most of the salesmen for the company work that into their sales presentation early, and sell it as a strong point.

But not this one fellow. He never even mentions the co-op advertising until he's down to the close. At that time, he says, "If you give me a thousand dollar order right now, today, I'll see that you get a hundred dollars co-op advertising money."

I asked this fellow what he'd do if the prospect replied, "You'd see that I got it if I waited 'til next month to place the order, too."

"Don't think that doesn't happen," he said. "And it doesn't bother me a bit. Here's my answer:

"I cannot, *cannot* promise you a hundred dollars co-op money if you put off ordering. There's a sharp difference of opinion among company executives about co-op budgets, and the co-op setup might be tossed out tomorrow. You can't tell. But today you can get that money, which is just like finding a hundred dollars."

Fewer Call-Backs

He needs fewer call-backs to close sales than any other man in his company.

One salesman watches his company's national spot television schedules closely. "During the next month," he tells the customer who wants to put off buying, "we're spending $300,000 on a heavy spot TV campaign. If I were you, I'd buy right now, to get the advantage of all that extra sales help."

Did I give logical benefits from immediate purchase?

Many companies furnish their salesmen with special inducements for immediate purchase. When you stop to consider the cost of a call-back, let alone the cost of losing an order, they can well afford to do it.

The management of one proprietary drug company shows great imagination in its special offers. One that cost little and got great results was a big sheet of perforated labels with adhesive on the back. Each label was to be put on the shelf carrying certain specific items, and each label carried the names of tie-in items that could be suggested by the salesman. For example, on the shelf that held shampoos, the label said, "Home Permanent, Wave Set, Hair Tint, Hair Creams, Electric Hair Dryers, Brush and Comb Sets, Hair Nets," and other items at some length. There was a label of similar nature for practically every shelf in a drug store.

System Was Not for Sale

"This tie-in suggestion system is not for sale," the salesman for the drug manufacturer was instructed to say. "You can't buy it at any price, but if you give me an order for one case of our antacid, you get the tie-in system absolutely free."

The extra inducement for immediate purchase didn't cost much, but it was a recognizable value to every druggist that saw it. And it did a fine job of increasing sales.

Some of the items used by manufacturers are really nothing more than premiums given in return for an immediate sale—things like desk clocks, pen and pencil sets, Thermos bottles, picnic hampers—items that don't cost much but have a definite appeal. They're a little added spur to action.

A refrigerator salesman I know pays for a little food deodorizer out of his own pocket, simply because he's found that offering one of them to a customer can help to prompt immediate action. He told me that they cost him 38 cents apiece in quantity. The other salesmen on the staff think he's crazy to spend the money, but, like Liberace, he laughs all the way to the bank.

On the retail floor, the "7 cents Off" coupon and similar approaches seem trivial, but they get results that are astounding. Apparently, they give the housewife just enough of a little nudge to impel buying action.

I remember a spur-for-action inducement that the Staley Company used for a number of years that had a double edge. At just the right time in spring, they offered free packets of flower seeds with Sta-Flo liquid laundry starch. The seeds came from a well-known seed company and gave the housewife an extra reason to pick up a bottle of liquid starch right then. There was the added incentive that if the seeds were going to be of any value, the housewife had to buy before it was too late to plant them.

Breakfast food companies have used constantly-changing premiums for years, finding little premium items that make children literally stir up a fuss to get immediate buying action from their mothers.

Attend a National Premium Show and you'll be amazed at the scope of the premium business. It's grown to such size because premiums have an *immediate* effect on sales in retail stores.

Of course, the size of the extra inducement depends on the size of the sale it's supposed to promote. If you're selling big ticket goods, a pack of flower seeds or a breakfast food premium probably wouldn't have much influence.

Flower Seeds—Free Trips to Florida

That's why a land promoter offers free trips to Florida to look at your new Florida lot purchase. He's playing for higher stakes and can afford to pay more for an immediate close.

A few years ago, I was doing some sales training work for a leading hot-water-heater manufacturer. The work hadn't really gotten well under way, I hasten to add.

Water heater sales were the slowest they had ever been in the history of the company, but management didn't lay off any help or shut

Did I give logical benefits from immediate purchase?

down any production lines. Heaters were coming off the line on regular schedule.

When all the warehouse space was full of heaters, management began looking around for extra storage space and found some.

Things actually reached the point where the aisles of this huge plant were filled with water heaters. There were even heaters in corridors. I've never seen so many heaters in my life and don't ever expect to see so many again. The company faced a crisis. Despite the slow sales on water heaters, most business was healthy, and there was a help problem in the community. Management felt that if men were laid off, they would go immediately to other companies and never come back. Nobody in the company liked the idea of shutting down, anyway.

Telephone Price Campaign

In a discussion that was getting nowhere, the sales manager finally said, "All right, let's quit talking and sell the heaters." Nobody thought it could be done, and the sales manager agreed that it would be hard to accomplish in a normal way. He had figures on what storage was costing the company, and since some heaters had been stored for 60 days, the cost was alarming.

He typed out a telephone sales solicitation and gave it to every executive in the firm, as well as to all his salesmen.

The whole sales talk was this: "If you'll let us ship you at least a dozen water heaters right now, today, you'll get 25% off your normal cost."

Retail sales were slow on heaters, but that price inducement got action. It prompted almost unbelievable sales. In two days, the glut of heaters at the factory was over. Apparently, nobody could resist such a bargain and such a chance to make extra money.

"Special price" doesn't take much imagination and it always costs money, but if you need results, it's one way you can nearly always get them in a hurry. It's a way, incidentally, that a real pro hates to use unless everything else has failed.

One sales manager has instructed his men in the field, when faced with "Wait 'til next month" to say, "If you'll place the order right now, you can get the goods immediately and we won't bill you 'til next month." The sales manager says, "What it amounts to is roughly a 2% discount for an order instead of a 'Come back next month and I'll see.' I don't encourage it, but it's helped business and increased company profits."

A furniture salesman in a "schlock" furniture company uses the ultimate "buy now" appeal. This company always has a few unadvertised specials that may not be very good merchandise but look like terrific values. They're "in-store leaders."

This salesman tells the customer, "If you buy right now,, I'm going to sweeten the deal. Along with the furniture you've picked out, you can buy this heavy-duty aluminum electric frypan for only $7.95. And you know what electric frypans usually cost."

We always had an overrun of the current month's issue of our newspaper advertising service. So our men used this buy-now inducement. "If you place your order for the service right now, while I'm here, I'll see that you get the current issue of the service absolutely free—a whole month's supply of mats, layouts, copy—the whole month's service. That means that if you buy today, you get 13 months service for the price of 12."

A Day of Demonstrating

A man who is something of a genius in the cosmetics field uses this routine when he's introducing a new item or calling on a new account.

He pulls a little book out of his pocket and studies it. "Let me see," he says. "Well, it looks like it would have to be within the next 10 days. If you'll place this order right now, I'll come in and do a full day of demonstrating for your customers." If the prospect asks, "Couldn't

Did I give logical benefits from immediate purchase?

you do the same thing a little later?" he answers, "Sorry, but I'll be clear out of this area and the company has me booked just about solid. But right now, I can do it."

A young salesman for another line of cosmetics doesn't show the attractive floor display. He waits until time to close and then says, "We have a beautiful floor display that goes with this offer. I think I still have one of them in my car. Let me see." The trip to look doesn't take him long. "We're in luck," he says, carting in the display. "If you place the order right now, I'll set up this display for you while I'm here. I know how to do it, and your men might have a little trouble with it."

Tips From Life Insurance

Life insurance salesmen are masters at using birthdates as spurs to close sales. If you pass a certain date, you pay a higher premium.

One insurance salesman, who had nothing else to offer as a spur to immediate action, gave me a little gem when I told him I'd like to think it over for a few days.

"Please, please don't do that," he said. "I'm not superstitious—at least, no more so than anybody else—but I've reached the conclusion that the surest way to court trouble is to be without insurance. I had one customer drop me a note instead of phoning and asking me to call on him. He was mad at the company that had his car insurance and he'd canceled it. Before the note asking me to call on him arrived, he had an accident that involved an $18,000 judgment against him. It practically wiped him out."

The Scientist said, "At one time, I worked out a list of six good reasons why a potential customer should buy from my company right now instead of waiting. Every reason of the six made good sense.

"Unfortunately, the barrage of six reasons didn't work at all. They didn't help me to close. I couldn't understand it.

"One of my men said, 'Maybe we're laying it on too thick. Do you suppose we're confusing people?'

"I didn't think so, but I'm always willing to check anything. So I said, 'Well, let's find out. Instead of the six reasons we've been using, let's determine the best of the six and use it.'

"We did, and closes picked up immediately. The men agreed that it worked. I still couldn't believe it, but the results were there. I finally said, 'All right, now let's try to close with the weakest of the six reasons we had instead of the best one.' We did, and results didn't decline enough to mean anything. The men still closed.

"We checked and double-checked and triple-checked from every angle. And we had to face the fact that one good reason for buying now was effective, where three or four good reasons were ineffective, and the six we'd started out with were hopeless.

"Maybe it's that the close becomes a matter of immediacy and a whole list of reasons requires thought and consideration for each one. In other words, they demand time on the customer's part. Whether that's a correct analysis or not, I do know that one quick reason works and any number of additional reasons delay the sale instead of speeding it up.

"I'd never thought a salesman could have too much ammunition— and I still don't believe it—but I know that *using* too much on Point 17 can kill you. So, of course, can using none."

Because of my interest in Point 17, I ask any salesman who tries to sell me anything if he can give me a reason why I should buy it right now.

"I Sure Could Use the Order"

You wouldn't believe the pitiful answers some salesmen come up with, after considerable fumbling around. The worse I've had recently was one, whose only recommendation was honesty. "Well," this salesman said, "I could sure use the order."

I really liked what an Abercrombie and Fitch salesman said when I told him I'd think awhile about buying the fly rod he'd shown me.

Did I give logical benefits from immediate purchase?

"I hope you don't lose too many fish while you're thinking it over," he grinned. "If you really intend to buy the rod, it'll last a lifetime— and you're cheating yourself out of pleasure every day you don't have it."

"Enjoy the Benefits Now"

A friend was looking at summer resort properties and I tagged along. He found a place, but couldn't bring himself to close the deal.

"When I bought my summer cottage," the salesman said, "my friends all told me I shouldn't barge into such a large luxury purchase. Well, property at that lake, the same site you're considering, went up 10% last year. My family has had the enjoyment of the place for eight years, and I could sell it today for about half again what I paid for it. We've had a lot of fun and it's been free. The friends who advised me to wait are still thinking it over. Furthermore, properties as good as the one you're looking at don't sit around long. It could very well be sold tomorrow."

My friend bought the place, and hasn't regretted it.

If you have gimmicks or price cuts, the inducement to immediate action is fairly easy, but a great many salesmen don't have such things.

Remember, you're selling benefits to the prospect, so you need to come up with a benefit he'll get from immediate purchase.

If you've sold the prospect the belief that purchase will be profitable to him, there's an obvious appeal. "You might as well start making money (or saving money) with this right now. The money you don't make tomorrow is gone forever."

If any of the benefits involve personal pleasure, a salesman can use this appeal. "This item will last you for years and you'll certainly enjoy it as long as you have it. Why not start enjoying it now instead of at some future time? It'll cost you the same, either way."

If economy is an important benefit to your prospect, you can always point out that prices have gone up and there's no assurance that they won't continue to do so. If you actually know of an impending price increase, you have a powerful action incentive.

If the big benefit to the buyer is Personal Importance or Prestige, it shouldn't be too difficult to show him that he can start enjoying that benefit right now at no greater cost than he'll pay to start enjoying it a month from now.

When a trade-in is involved in the sale, as in the case of a new automobile, the salesman can say, "Today, I think I have a good prospect for your old car, so I can give you a little more for it than I could have a week ago when the used-car business was slow. What I could offer for it next week, I simply don't know. It depends on the market, which hasn't been too dependable this year."

One way or another, you give the customer logical reasons for buying action right now, today.

Of the benefits you're selling in your product or service, which ones lend themselves to promoting immediate purchase?

Aside from what the company can offer in the way of inducements, is there anything you, yourself, can offer—as in the example of the cosmetics salesman who offered to stage a one-day product demonstration?

It must be most tactfully worded or it sounds terrible—but could you use the threat of selling a competitor if your prospect doesn't give you an immediate order?

Is there any shortage or delivery problem that makes an immediate order logical?

Is what you're selling an item or service that your prospect needs immediately?

Find all the spurs to immediate action you can—and then use the one that fits each situation best. Point 17 is a big step toward closing a sale.

18. Did I make a proper summary of the points that should influence purchase?

When you make a sales call, everything you do leads, hopefully, to getting the order. You sell benefits, selling hardest on those that you think will be most appealing to this particular prospect.

If your sales solicitation is any good at all, it has proved those benefits one at a time, step by step. In Point 17, you have just slanted a benefit toward immediate purchase rather than at some vague later date.

Sure, you've told the buyer everything you think should make him buy. So now, if you need to, you tell him again.

Only this time, you do it in summary form. If he's listened to your solicitation up to now, you don't need the explanations you used the first time around.

The summary is the quick, hard-hitting nailing of the lid onto the sale—bang, bang, bang!

Quite often, you'll get a definite indication that you should go to Point 19, the close, before you get to the summary. In that case, you don't need it. You're all set for your sale without taking up any more of the prospect's time.

But if you have *not* gotten that definite indication which we'll discuss when we get to Point 19, you better go right into your summary and it better be good. There's something that needs more emphasis, and the summary will hit it.

A good summary often takes longer to prepare than any other part of the sales solicitation—but it should *never* take long in actual performance. Conciseness is a must.

"Mr. Jones," you say, "you've agreed that this product will save you money, paying for itself in a few months. From that time forward, it will make money for you, as long as you have it. I think we're in agreement that Model 62 best fits your needs. You made a good choice of color. From what you've said, I think you understand and appreciate the convenience that Model 62 will bring to you. You certainly can be proud of owning it, and we went into the specifications thoroughly enough so that there shouldn't be any question about its durability or performance. You know that our company has a great reputation for service on everything we sell. I don't want to put words into your mouth, but aren't we in agreement on the things I'm talking about?"

If the answer is "No" on any point, you've just been saved by the bell. The summary has given you an opportunity to sell what evidently wasn't sold enough back in the main body of your talk.

If your solicitation has been thorough, detailed, and complicated, a prospect doesn't always remember every pearl of wisdom that dropped from your lips. Maybe he's forgotten an important one. And maybe he simply doesn't realize all the benefits that will accrue to him from purchase of your product until he hears them summarized, one right after the other, instead of hearing them discussed one at a time.

Emphasize Purchase Points

As a general rule of thumb, the longer your sales solicitation takes, the greater the chance is that you need to summarize before you close.

To keep your summary as hard-hitting as possible, you eliminate things that the prospect dismissed as of no consequence to him at the time you explained them. You summarize the things that you feel will prompt him to buy.

Did I make a proper summary of the purchase points?

I have heard summaries that were interminably long. More than one salesman has tired me out with a poorly prepared, disorganized summation of benefits, some of which didn't apply in any way to me or my problems.

Where you used shotgun shells in the body of your solicitation, now you should be using a machine-gun technique.

At the start, I told you that it's always been a problem to keep my eagerness to close from becoming too apparent too early. Well, at this point your eagerness to make a sale *should* begin to show. This customer wants or needs something that you want to sell. You've come to like him during your time with him, and you want this new friend to have the benefits you can bring him.

The sales manager of a large appliance store has a neatly lettered card in every department. It is a summary of the benefits a specific appliance can bring to its users, along with a capsule explanation of what feature develops that benefit.

I asked this sales manager why he went to the expense of having these cards printed. "Because some of the summaries my men were using were just awful," he said. "They left out things that should have been emphasized and sometimes made practically another sales presentation instead of a summary, because they just plain didn't know how to be brief."

"Now," he continued, "they use the card. It keeps them from being too long-winded—and the card stays out in the customer's view until the sale is closed. The men all admit that the cards have been a great thing for them."

A good specialty salesman who called on me got to the summary point and pulled a piece of scratch paper out of his pocket. He printed on the paper:

Economy—$40-$50 a week saving.
Convenience—20 hours a week time saved.
Quality.
Minimum service.

He mentioned each benefit as he wrote. And just as he was finishing his summary, he tossed the sheet of paper to my side of the desk, turning it so the words faced me. Without seeming to use a mechanized tool, he had that summary under my nose all during his effort to close.

Later, visiting with him, I said, "That was a good selling trick you used—that summary on the scratch paper. Did you ever think of having it neatly printed on a little card?"

"Yes," he said, "but it wouldn't work for me. You see, I try to fit the summary to the man. You'll remember that I skipped quite a few things with you, because I'd seen that they didn't interest you. Anyway, this seems so much more casual and personal. I don't think I'd feel comfortable with a printed card."

I always try to include Point 10 in any summary I make. To me, Point 10 is as strong a selling weapon as you can have. I've often closed a sale right at Point 10 without continuing—but if I don't, I certainly try to make the most of it in the summary.

Probably the most daring summary I ever heard was given by a young man whose job was to sell 10 acres of ground to a school board for $100,000. He really staked his entire summary on Point 10.

The Blunt Truth Worked

He had some hot competition, but when his turn came to try to close, he said to the board, "I could talk about the logic of this location, its convenience, what it will save in bus mileage—I could go on and on. But I don't intend to. The ground I'm offering you is the only location for a high school in this entire district that makes sense. You can consider the other locations from now to kingdom come, but you will finally face the fact that the taxpayers of this community *want* this location. They think it's the only one worth considering. They'll be mighty unhappy if you buy any other ground. You know it and I know it. The price is higher than the others because this is desirable property and the other offerings aren't. It's worth the difference. All

Did I make a proper summary of the purchase points?

I really want to say in my summary is that if this property is your final choice, you'll be reelected. If it isn't, you won't be. Thank you."

The members of the school board didn't like the blunt way he put it, but they knew what he'd told them was true. After only a few minutes' deliberation, the president of the board said, "Well, you heard what Joe Hanks said. I didn't like the way he put it, but I do want to be reelected—and I'd like to entertain a motion that we buy this property."

The motion was unanimously approved, and Joe Hanks had been right in betting everything on Point 10.

In making your summary, you assume that you've already proved your points. You speak as if the prospect had agreed with you. Your summary points can be emphatic, worded more strongly than they were when you first presented them. The prospect expects you to be positive now—and if he questions anything you say, he'll let you know.

An acquaintance of mine had to sell a state Chamber of Commerce board and was one of six finalists chosen to give a summary presentation. The other five advertising agencies who were after the account were to preceed him in the meeting, and he knew that the board members would be weary by the time he got to talk.

His Summary, a Newspaper Ad

He took a full-page ad in the afternoon newspaper, which he knew would hit the street while the meeting was in progress. The ad was his summary, over the logotype of his agency.

When the time came for him to speak, he entered the conference room with a dozen copies of the paper.

"Gentlemen," he said, "I happen to believe in what I'm selling— advertising. I don't know whether the other agencies who are after your business believe in it or not—for themselves, that is. But I do.

I believe in it enough and in its power to sell so that I've put my entire case into one newspaper ad. Go ahead and read it."

He passed out the papers to the board members and walked out of the room.

Daring? It certainly was, but it was sound and different. He got the account.

Blizzards Don't Sell in the South

A similar case involved a late uncle of mine, W. C. Newton, who was a great advertising salesman. He knew that a tourist state was looking for an advertising agency. He didn't happen to have an agency, but the account was worth several million dollars' billing, and he could figure 15% of that amount without too much effort. He worked diligently to get the account, competing against some New York agencies who had everything to offer in the way of agency services.

He based his entire sales approach on his being in the state, knowing its problems, and being able to give the account his undivided personal attention—which, he contended, the big New York agencies couldn't do.

It was a Southern state; the time, the middle of winter. Basking in the warm sun on the morning of the summations, he picked up the local newspaper. On page two there was a half-page ad which said, "When a blizzard rages outside, light up a Blanko cigarette and enjoy yourself." The art work showed a couple sitting in front of a beautiful fireplace, and a big picture window framed the blizzard outside.

He had prepared a gem of a summation, which he knew he was going to have to do fast to get it into the one hour allotted to him. He also knew that the ad he'd just read had been prepared and placed by the one major agency that was still solidly in the running.

He abandoned the summary presentation in which he had six hundred dollars invested, and bought a dozen copies of the paper. When

Did I make a proper summary of the purchase points?

his turn came, he walked into the room and passed out the papers, opened to page 2.

"Gentlemen," he said, "I have a strong feeling that the competition for this account has narrowed down to the Bigshot Agency and myself. I've told you all along that I'm right here, know your problems, and can solve them better than an outsider. The ad you're looking at was prepared by the Bigshot Agency. It's a beautiful, well-executed ad. The space in this particular paper, in this city, cost the cigarette company $174.28. That's the client's money, just as it will be your money that I or they spend on your advertising. Now, I have just one question—how many of you gentlemen have ever seen a blizzard?" Two of the 12 men held up their hands. The rest were natives of the state, as my uncle well knew.

"Thank you, gentlemen," he said. "If you want your money spent this way, I'll abide by your decision. But I don't think you do. I rest my case."

He made the sale, and later told me he was positive that if he had used his beautiful one-hour summary, he'd have lost it.

"I knew the big agency could outsell me on everything except one benefit," he admitted. "That happened to be a desirable benefit, and it was one the big agency couldn't offer. I was lucky to find such a beautiful way to dramatize it."

If you have only one benefit to sell, that's your summary.

Exact Words Not Important

The Personality Kid sales manager says of the summary, "My first boss sold me on the tremendous importance of it. He made me feel that the summary was the thing that got the order.

"A few years ago, I began taping the summaries used by my men, and they were good ones. Sometimes they got orders and sometimes they didn't. I was forced to this conclusion: it isn't the summary but the way the salesman handles it that gets business.

"You can have the sharpest summary ever devised, and the customer will be impressed by it, but it won't sell a dime's worth of business by itself. You have to revise it almost every time you use it, to fit squarely into a selling situation. You can start with a readymade summary but somewhere along the line you have to make alterations to get business.

"For example, I have one pet customer. After I've gone through the benefits on anything I'm selling him, I can always tell which one he's bought. When it comes time for the summary, I summarize that one benefit and forget everything else. It always works, and I have a feeling that if I were to go over every point I've previously mentioned, the man would walk away from me. He appreciates that I sense his feelings and don't waste time on anything except his major interest.

His Advice—"Stay Loose"

"Then I have another customer who's entirely different. I summarize every benefit for him. If I didn't, this fellow would feel that he was being shortchanged. He wants a mental file of all the reasons why he should buy.

"It's easy for a salesman to get the idea that his summary is almost automatic—that it's one of the few places in the sales presentation where no thought or judgment is required. Well, he couldn't be more wrong."

My own criticism of summaries is that so many of them are dull, and they don't have to be. Could your summary be shortened without impairing its effectiveness? Is there any way you could pep it up? Have you worked out ways of emphasizing the points that will count most with each prospective buyer? Are you "loose" enough to make on-the-spot changes in it?

Do you feel awkward doing a summary? Some salesmen do. One really fine salesman confessed to me that he always felt like a member of the high-school debating team when he reached the summary.

Did I make a proper summary of the purchase points?

If you feel awkward about it, you must face the fact that your summary isn't well planned. There's nothing at all awkward about a carefully thought-out summary. It should fit in naturally at the proper time.

In conscientiously trying to condense their summaries, some men put the points into words that are entirely different from their normal conversation. You can't do that and get away with it. It's better to take another minute or two than to sound like you're prattling something written for you by somebody else—somebody who doesn't know how you talk.

Make it hit quickly but hard. Assume agreement on every point until you're corrected, but give the prospect a chance to correct you. Then go into that point fully enough to *get* agreement.

It's often helpful to prepare a summary on some product other than the one you're selling. You can be so close to your own product or service that you don't really know what your summary points are.

You need the summary most on the most difficult sales—and on the really tough ones, the summary does your most effective selling.

19. Did I make a definite, direct appeal for the order at the proper time?

"At the proper time" is the catch on Point 19. Salesmen almost automatically ask, when they hear the point, "But what *is* the proper time?"

There's a simple answer to the question. Unfortunately, most salesmen don't really understand the answer until it's amplified.

The proper time to close is when the seller's and buyer's viewpoints have merged.

You begin a sales solicitation knowing that the completion of the sale will be advantageous to you.

The potential buyer starts listening to your sales solicitation not knowing whether or not the purchase of your product or service will be beneficial to him.

Somewhere along the line, if a sale is ever going to be closed, you and the buyer feel that here is a mutually advantageous transaction. The buyer, of course, doesn't care about how advantageous it is for you.

In a few cases, the prospect has actually made up his mind that he's going to buy before you call on him. He wants a little information to confirm his prejudgment and presto, the viewpoints have merged.

Sometimes a prospect wants to buy but hasn't made up his mind who should get the order. By the end of the personal points, the viewpoints should have merged.

Did I make a direct appeal for the order at the proper time?

More often, the man wants proof—if only to confirm his preconceived judgment. When he gets the part of the proof that has bothered him, he's all set.

On some occasions, your interests and the prospect's interests are almost diametrically opposite at the start. You are interested in getting his money in exchange for the goods, and he is interested in avoiding anything that may cost him money.

You're interested in self benefit and so is he—but he isn't at all sure that buying what you're selling will benefit him in the slightest. He knows, on the other hand, that holding onto his money is pleasant.

Somewhere along the line, you and your prospect get together. Often it is so apparent that there's no question about it.

You aim toward a close right from the start, point by point. You not only aim but you build toward a close. You start out by making a favorable impression on the customer. You talk from the customer's viewpoint. The instant he recognizes that you're taking his viewpoint, he may make it clear that the two viewpoints have merged. Without having presented any real proof, this may be the time to close.

Then you find the basic need or desire on the customer's part and try to capitalize on it. He may accept this eagerly. You've come together, so you try to close.

He may show that he's in the market for your product and thinks your company is the greatest. So why wait? You close.

Close When Ready

You tell the customer some new beneficial thing about your product or service that he didn't already know. He then shows you that this has put him on your side, with your viewpoint. A sale will be beneficial to both of you. So you close.

You show the customer all the advantages to him of buying your product. If he says, "Yes, I can see that," you close.

You show him an advantage he can't obtain from any other source. He says, in effect, "Yes, I want that benefit." So you ask him for his order.

He shows that he's tremendously influenced by the endorsement of some particular person—somebody he respects. He sees that he, too, can benefit from buying. So you ask for the order.

He admits that you've answered his only objections to his complete satisfaction. You're now both on the same side of the fence, all ready to benefit, so you close the sale.

Wait for Another Opening

But what if you guess wrong on the meeting of minds? What if you try to close too early? You aren't defeated. You just continue right along with the solicitation until the time when the two viewpoints *do* merge. At that point, a sale can be closed.

But if you were wrong on your first guess, how do you tell when the point of agreement really occurs?

First, the prospect tells you. That is, he tells you if you watch and listen. He seldom says it in so many words, but he indicates it. Sometimes he indicates it before he consciously realizes that he's ready to buy.

But what about old Stone Face, who *doesn't* tell you? You ask him. For example, let's take Point 10—the exclusive benefit. You say, "We're mighty proud of this feature which nobody else has. Tell me, honestly, is it important to you?"

If he says that it is, you follow up with, "Well, since nobody else has it and it's important to you, let's fill out the order."

If you've gone clear through to the summary without getting a sale, you must do everything you can to get approval of the summation—and then you must ask for the order immediately.

A certain automobile salesman conditions his prospect to the close. He has an order pad in his hand from the start of his sales story. He

Did I make a direct appeal for the order at the proper time?

says, "Well, I think we're agreed that this would be the best model for you, aren't we?" And when he gets a "Yes," he writes the model designation on the order blank. One of the benefits he's selling is appearance—beauty—Personal Importance. After he's shown the color combinations and the upholstery choices, he asks the prospect which ones he thinks are most attractive. And he writes the answer on the order blank.

When he feels it's time to close, he looks at the order blank and holds it out to the customer. "That's funny," he says. "I made notes on what you wanted, while we were looking and talking—and what it amounts to is a completed order, all ready to sign."

The salesman who makes a blunt demand, barging in, hammer and tongs, usually gets rebuffed. Few prospects like to feel that they're being bullied.

It's almost a tossup between the bully and the Timid Soul who apologizes when he asks for the order—but I'd have to give the bully the nod. I had one timid fellow ask me the other day, "Do you think maybe you'd like to sign an order for this, or would you rather think it over for a few days?"

When you ask the price, one salesman says, "Well, it will depend on what extras you want. Of course, you don't have to take any of them, but I believe some of them would be a big help to you."

He starts making out an order, then and there. When the price has been arrived at, he holds the order out to the customer. "There it is," he says, "all ready to sign."

The "Customer's Choice" Close

Some salesmen make filling out an order blank look like an effort to help the customer to decide on the right thing. It can be great or it can look like pure pressure, depending on how it's handled.

Proper handling is the secret of another closing technique, the "customer's choice." It can do a tremendous job. Do it crudely and it be-

205

comes a "Have you stopped beating your wife?" kind of question which the customer deeply resents.

The technique is to ask the customer to make a choice. Ideally, it's an attractive choice you offer, as opposed to a less attractive one.

One time, the salesman for a New York television station asked me if I'd do him a favor. "I offered one of your accounts a spot in Million Dollar Movie," he explained. "It's roughly a hundred thousand dollar package. The man seems to be interested but he won't give me an order. I've made four calls on him and I've reached the point where I don't much care whether I get a yes or no. I can't get either one, and I don't want to make a career out of trying. Would you see if you could get him to say yes or no?"

I agreed to try—and I did try. Boy, how I tried. And I got not one inch farther than the TV station representative had gotten. His information to me had been quite right—my client was genuinely interested. It was apparent that he wanted the TV ad package, but he simply would not place an order.

I had flown to the city where his plant was located, arriving at 9:30 a.m. We talked until noon. I went over every detail of the program. I summarized briefly, and then I summarized in detail, without getting anything even close to a buying decision. We went to lunch and came back to his office. I virtually started all over again, with no better results.

Finally, I looked at my watch. "Say," I said, "I'm scheduled for a 4 o'clock plane for Chicago and if I don't get moving, I'll miss it."

"You sure will," he nodded. "I'll have the girl call you a cab right this minute. You'll have to hurry."

I put on my hat and coat, closed my briefcase and got ready to leave. As I reached the office door, I turned around. "Harold," I asked, "what do you want to do? Do you want me to come back down here Monday and go over this whole thing again, or do you want to buy it right now?"

"Oh," he said, "I guess I'll buy it now."

Did I make a direct appeal for the order at the proper time?

I still shudder thinking of how close I came to missing a hundred thousand dollar order. The customer's choice question did the job. Harold didn't really want to go through another whole day of listening to the proposal any more than I did. And of course, he really did want the advertising package. I would have done both him and myself a great disfavor if I hadn't asked that one last question.

A vacuum cleaner salesman did a good job with the "customer's choice" technique when he said to my wife, "There's no difference in the efficiency of the upright model and the tank model. Which do you prefer?"

"The tank model," my wife answered.

"Fine," the salesman nodded, and then, assuming that she'd ordered it, continued, "That's the one we'll specify in the order, then."

I'll be darned if my wife didn't nod approvingly, without any thought that she'd been pressured into a close.

He had a much better "customer's choice" question for himself than the one I'd given my customer of buying now or having me spend another day with him. Whichever choice my wife made, this fellow was going to benefit.

I heard a salesman ask a factory manager, "If you buy, would you want immediate delivery or would you want it held up until next month?"

"I'd want it held up until after the first," the man said.

A Leading Question

"Fine," the salesman said, "I'll make out the order that way." He did, and the factory manager signed it.

If your personality doesn't lend itself to the point-blank request for an order, questions, even without a choice, seem to have much lower pressure involved in them.

"Would you like to start cutting your bookkeeping costs right now?" a salesman asked a prospect. The answer was "Yes." "Then," the salesman said, "we better make out the order."

One that I thought was weak but got results was the question an insurance salesman asked me. "Can you think of any reason," he demanded, "why you shouldn't start enjoying the protection of this insurance today?" I was tempted to throw a curve at him and answer, "Yes, I can think of four reasons." But I wanted the insurance, so he closed the sale.

Warning—Don't "Unclose"

A friend confided, laughing, how a salesman asked his wife the perfect closer. "My wife and her sister have a buying competition," he explained. "If one gets anything, the other has to have it. Well, it came out in the course of this guy's sales pitch that the company had sold a color TV set to Linnie's sister. And when he got ready to close, he asked my wife, 'Don't you think that this is a good time to start enjoying the quality TV performance that your sister has in her home?' My wife snapped, 'I certainly do—but I want a little nicer cabinet.' He had the one perfect closer for Linnie."

You waste a great deal of your working life if you don't ask for the order. There's no mysterious magic moment when the sale can be closed. There may be eight or nine different times when you can get the order. If you miss on one, try the next.

Ideally, the prospect says something that almost waves a flag in your face with the word "Close" on it. And if you're wrong right up to the conclusion of the summary, you still have an opportunity to make your do-or-die effort.

Here's a warning that seems ridiculously unnecessary—but isn't. Don't unclose after you've closed a sale.

It's been done plenty of times. I have a horrible memory of an advertising new-business man who sold a million-dollar account. He

Did I make a direct appeal for the order at the proper time?

sold it. The chairman of the board agreed that this was his new advertising agency.

Then Humphrey said, "Mr. Sage, you've made a wise decision. To show you how wise it is, here's the first thing we're going to do for you." He hastily outlined a fuzzy merchandising plan.

"We tried that four years ago," Mr. Sage said, "and lost our shirts on it."

"But that's just a beginning," Humphrey persisted. In 10 minutes of fast talking, he completely unsold Mr. Sage who, in ushering him out the door said, "I guess we better think it over. We'll let you know when we're ready for another talk."

Even oftener, the customer has done everything except plead for the order blank, but the salesman keeps right on talking, selling, talking some more until he's worn out the would-be customer—and alienated him in the process.

Once I went along with a salesman who put on a really good two-hour presentation. He got worried because the man who was going to do the buying got the fidgets. The fellow squirmed and twisted and turned. He got up and paced back and forth.

The salesman felt he must not be working hard enough, so he bore down on his summary. He spelled it out in detail. By the time he asked for the order, the prospect said, "Uh—could you wait awhile? If you'll excuse me for five minutes . . ."

When You "Gotta Go"

My man *wouldn't* excuse him. He was determined not to let that prospect get away.

The prospect said, "No, I am not going to sign an order right now. As I've now told you three times, I'll discuss it with you if you excuse me for five minutes. On second thought, you don't need to excuse me. Wait here." And he stalked out of the room.

"What's wrong with this nut?" the salesman asked me.

"Bob," I said, "he's needed desperately to go to the toilet for nearly half an hour. I'm afraid that he's mad at you now for not letting him do it."

"I'll be darned," Bob said. "Why didn't he say so?"

Well, there are people, particularly older men, who won't say so. I don't know whether it's through some Victorian modesty or because they think admission of their normal bodily functions is a sign of weakness.

Whatever the reason, when you see a prospect get the squirms after sitting through a long presentation, don't try to close the sale. Suggest a short break and *then* ask for the order.

The Obsolete Product

You've never had it happen? Well, I have, enough times to think it's worth mentioning. We want to eliminate *every*thing that might keep you from closing.

Nobody likes to inject a sour note into a beautiful selling symphony, but The Roughneck came up with a dandy, and, in fairness, it must be recognized.

He said, "When you ask yourself, 'Did I ask for the order at the proper time,' your answer on some products has to be 'No—the proper time was four years ago' or 'No—there's never going to be a proper time.'

"What I'm getting at," he continued, "is that sometimes a salesman is saddled with an item that just isn't salable. He has to buck the current trend, and there's nothing harder to do.

"I've seen companies keep an item on the market five years after it was obsolete—and raise hell with their salesmen because they didn't bring in orders. I've seen other companies market a new half-baked product that you couldn't give away—a product that was never consumer-tested by anyone except the company president's wife.

Did I make a direct appeal for the order at the proper time?

"I've seen other products that were so overpriced you had to hunt for idiots if you wanted to make any sales—and you weren't even going to find many of them stupid enough to buy.

"I've seen poor devils trying to sell a line of cars whose styling was completely outdated. I've seen salesmen trying to get back in after a manufacturer had gotten all his dealers into trouble with a succession of rotten products and worse make-good performance.

"Not even a top-notch pro can close in situations like those. The difference between the hot pro and the amateur, though, is that the real pro won't *try* to close after he finds what's wrong. He'll get out and get another job where he has something to sell. The amateur will keep trying, taking a beating from the office and from the prospects until the company can't afford to pay him any longer. He's so horse-whipped by that time that he probably won't ever be a good salesman."

Study Assignments for You

Let's hope that there's a ready market for what you're selling. Come up with some examples of how you might handle:

1. The "customer's choice" technique.

2. The indirect-question closing.

3. The order-blank technique.

4. The direct request for the order.

20. Did I leave the door open for a successful call-back or resale?

We debated a long time about Point 20 and finally agreed that it belonged in any theoretically perfect selling plan.

You already know that there are times when you don't make a sale. On some products and services, you're doing well if you close one out of five on the first call.

Your objective is to sell—so if you don't do it on the first call, it's a basic part of good selling to make the prospect want you to come back for further discussion.

There are always ways to come up with a reason for coming back. I once made a call where I didn't get to first base because the prospect had one violent objection that I couldn't overcome. I thought my logic was fine, but this customer was completely unimpressed. He was courteous and interested—but he didn't for one minute buy my answer to his objection. Every time I tried to close him, he went back to it, and he finally said, "Young man, you're wasting your time trying to sell me until you have a satisfactory answer to my one objection."

As I was about to leave his office, I turned and said, "You know, your objection is an important one. If the way I've been told to handle it doesn't stand up, I want to know if there *is* a good answer to it. I'm going directly to the president of the company to get his explanation, and if it makes sense, I'll be back in a day or so."

I went to the president and reported everything that had happened. "The sales training people told you to say *what*?", he demanded incredulously. "You mean that's the answer our salesmen are all giving on that point? The man you tried to sell was right. It *doesn't* stand up. No wonder we're losing sales."

He was so incensed that he made the call-back with me, which greatly impressed the prospect. It took the two men about 10 minutes to agree on what had been a hopeless stumbling block, and I got the order.

Every salesman has a tendency to lose his cool when he fails to close. There's sometimes a tremendous temptation to tell off a prospect you feel has been unreasonable—and it's never yet paid off in anything except a shallow and fleeting self-satisfaction.

Whether you make a sale or not, you keep the door open.

Originally, a point in our system for selling was, "Was my timing right on this call?" Two of the sales managers felt strongly that timing was tremendously important—and I concurred.

My background included a great deal of selling in radio and television. To sell a show, you had to find an agency and sponsor who were in the market. You could have the greatest show in the world and could get clients to agree with you—but if they weren't ready to break with a show, you weren't going to sell them. That's one of several reasons why there are more good shows off the air than on— but let's not get into that.

Timing *Is* Important

The Scientist was adamant that timing should *not* be one of the points. "What we're trying to build," he said, "is a perfect sales presentation from opening to close. Timing is something that's determined or happens before the solicitation is made. You have no control over it. In many instances, you can't possibly know if you're striking at the right time. I'll grant you that timing affects sales, but it isn't a part of the solicitation."

The three of us finally had to admit, grudgingly, that The Scientist was right.

Then he turned around and agreed with us that timing should be a factor in Point 20. "In considering a call-back to try to close a sale," he said, "timing becomes a controllable. You now know the prospect's objections. You can have some control over the timing of a call-back. So as a part of the question, 'Did I leave the door open for a call-back?' you can also ask yourself, 'What should be the timing of that next call?' "

Unfortunately, the timing of your call is often pure chance. If it's right, you make a sale without any great effort. If it's wrong, you can be the greatest salesman in the world and you're not going to close— on this trip.

Sometimes on a Silver Platter

Advertising agencies have gone after new accounts with simply great creative work—and have scarcely made a dent on the client they were after.

Then an agency with less to offer has called on the account a month or two later—at a time when the agency of record is having trouble with the account—and has had a large piece of billing practically handed to it on a silver platter. You can try to analyze such situations —and sometimes your feeling that strange things are happening proves to be right—but you can't really know in advance.

There's not nearly as much luck in selling as the amateur salesman likes to believe—but often timing *is* a matter of chance. In some cases, a salesman is regarded as an expert only because he happened to be in the right place at the right time. Don't knock it. If you can come up with that kind of luck, you can be regarded as a sales genius.

On the question of timing, ask yourself in planning a call-back, "What are the factors that will influence this man's purchase?" There may be things over which you have no control—like available money, an increasing need for the product or service, approval of expansion by a board of directors, pressure from competition—all kinds of things.

Did I leave the door open for a successful call-back?

Once you've recognized the factors, watch for a favorable time and then get in there in a hurry. When you can time a sales call right, you're in like the proverbial Mr. Flynn.

But there are other things to be considered in call-backs. One company insists that every salesman call back two weeks after the product is delivered, to see if everything is all right. This company makes high-priced items, and once it gets a product in, its history is that it gets the whole line in, sooner or later.

If you're calling back because you failed to make a sale, it shouldn't be too difficult to find out why. Then you ask yourself how you can correct whatever was wrong. When you've determined that, you go back and sometimes what was an impossible first call becomes a quick, easy sale on the second.

Let's be honest, though. Sometimes it doesn't. If you wind up firm in the belief that you've finally done everything right, you don't waste any more time on a no-sale account until you think you have a new approach. You devote your time, instead, to calls where you seem to have a chance.

Once I made a new business call where I completely failed to determine the customer's major interests. I couldn't have made a worse approach if I'd deliberately tried. And I didn't realize how wrong I'd been until after the summary. I still asked for the order, but devoted more effort to Point 20, leaving the door open for a call-back.

Turned Around Too Quickly

By the time I left the prospect's office, I not only knew how wrong I'd been but where I'd goofed.

Then I made a second error. I went right back the next day and did a sales solicitation that was almost diametrically opposite to the first one.

"Young man," the fellow said, "what are you, a chameleon? The service you're selling has to be one thing or another. It can't have

215

changed completely overnight. People don't buy one patent medicine any more to cure everything from ringworm to a broken back."

Actually, the service I was selling would have done everything I claimed for it on the second call—but that wasn't believable to the customer. Looking back, I can't blame him for his skepticism.

So I began paying for my errors. I made a whole series of short, casual calls over a period of weeks, selling just one benefit on each call but trying to make it believable. It took me over three months to get the order.

Call-Back After a Sale

The call-back after you make a sale is at least as important as the call-back where you weren't able to close. Every sale can be and should be the beginning of a continuing profitable association. If you sell more than one item, the man you've conditioned is a much easier prospect for other goods than a stranger. Remember, he wants to buy from people he likes.

If I'm driving and come to a plant where I've sold something at one time or another, I drop in for a few minutes and maybe do nothing more than say hello and ask how things are going. Executives in out-lying plants are nearly always delighted to have this happen. It tells them that you like them and it shows that you have an interest in them. That can't ever annoy anybody.

Let's think about that from the customer's viewpoint. There was a television film salesman I genuinely liked. On the few occasions where I could, I tried hard to place business with him rather than with his competitors, and he was a buddy who dropped in for purely social calls with considerable frequency. Then I got into a position where I had only one television account, and its purchases were sewed up by one company as far as film was concerned. My old friend quit dropping in. It seemed to me that he avoided me.

A few competitive salesmen who knew the situation continued to drop around for visits—to tell me what they were doing and ask what

Did I leave the door open for a successful call-back?

was happening with me. My mental reaction soon became, "If Old Buddy's forgotten me, I can forget him, too."

While I had no business to give out, I did run across a couple of tips on extremely good business, one a situation where I could help. And it wasn't Old Buddy I helped. I don't believe I behaved any differently than most customers would.

The mail-order experts tell me that when somebody gives them an initial order, they're delighted to add that name to their mailing list. "It's the followup sales where you make your real money," they explain. "A person who has already bought something from a mail-order company becomes a 'live one,' and you aren't paying a penny for a good new name."

There's another great reason for the call-back after the completed sale. I've never known a salesman who didn't complain about the quality of the leads his employer gave him.

Good prospects are, of course, the life blood of a salesman's existence. So where is he going to get good leads? About the best place I know of is from the man who's already a customer.

For one thing, your customer knows who among his professional and personal friends would legitimately be in the market for what you're selling. He usually knows the financial condition of those friends. Psychology is working for you, too. Since this customer has bought your product or service, he'd like to have his friends following in his footsteps. He loves to think that he's influenced a friend. In the same vein, the prospect you get from a customer nearly always wants to maintain status on a par with that customer.

Prospects Lead to Prospects

I heard one salesman talking to another at a sales seminar. "You seem to get a lot of prospects from your customers," one said. "How in the devil do you do it?"

And the second salesman answered, "I ask."

"Well, how?" the first salesman persisted.

"Just plain out-and-out ask," Number Two said. "I usually lead off by saying, 'Mr. Blank, you can do me a big favor—and you might be doing your friends a favor, too.'"

"Isn't that kind of nervy?" the first salesman asked, "to ask a man you've sold to give you leads?"

"Nuts," Number Two said. "It strengthens our friendship. It doesn't cost him anything to give me leads, and people like to do favors for you unless a favor involves a lot of trouble."

Three Reasons for Point 20

There are three purposes to Point 20.

1. It keeps you from giving up on a prospect just because you didn't sell him on your first call.

2. It makes an initial sale result in more sales.

3. It gets you good leads on other potential buyers.

To stimulate your thinking on Point 20, what factors of timing have you ever encountered that would determine the time for a call-back?

What would be the best approach you could make on a call-back where you've already made a sale?

If you failed to make a sale on the first call because, in your opinion, the prospect didn't like you, how would you handle a call-back?

If you felt that he did like you on the first call but he still didn't buy, what would you do differently on a call-back?

In a sales seminar, I bore down hard on getting new business from call-backs on customers. A salesman protested, "But if I only made one sale a day and follow up to try to get more business, in a hundred days I'd have a hundred steady customers and I'd be so busy I wouldn't have any time to work on new business."

If that's bad, it's the kind of catastrophe I'd like to have happen to me—and to you.

Profitable Followthrough

You now have your own 20-Point Checklist. It reads like this:

Personal

1. Did I make a favorable impression on the customer?
2. Did I talk from the customer's viewpoint?
3. Did I find the basic desire or need on the part of the customer and then capitalize on it?
4. Did I encourage the customer to do part of the talking?
5. Did I give the customer any reason for coming back to me rather than to another salesman?

Proof

6. Did I properly convey the background and merits of the company?
7. Was I able to tell the customer at least one new beneficial thing about the product?
8. Was the customer thoroughly acquainted with all the advantages of the product or service by the time I concluded my solicitation?
9. Did I make the customer participate in the demonstration?
10. Did I offer the customer at least one advantage he could not obtain from any other source?
11. Did I prove the endorsement of others?
12. Did I use my company's sales aids to the best advantage?

Opposition

13. Did I overcome customer objection without encouraging argument?
14. Did I do a positive job of selling all the way?

15. Did I avoid letting the customer get me off the main sales line?

16. Did I encourage the customer to ask questions and did I answer them intelligently?

The Close

17. Did I give the customer logical reasons why he would benefit from immediate purchase?

18. Did I make a proper summary of the points that should influence purchase of the product?

19. Did I make a definite, direct appeal for the order at the proper time?

20. Did I leave the way open for a successful call-back or resale?

The points won't do you any good unless you fit them to your situation—your personality, your product or service, and your prospective customers.

Examine the list of 20 points critically. Every point makes sense, doesn't it? Unless you're one in a million, you will have to admit that some points of the 20 have been neglected in your selling and a few haven't ever been a part of any solicitation you've made.

The man who knows all the fundamentals and how to apply them can sell anything, tangible or intangible. He doesn't have to stake everything on statistics, because he knows how to sell.

When you've checked yourself on the 20 Points for a month, you'll know them well enough so that you can start checking yourself on the four major *divisions* of the points:

PERSONAL

PROOF

OPPOSITION

CLOSE

You'll be able to question yourself on any division and know instantly what points in that division you flunked.

Little has been said here about Personal Enthusiasm—which any good salesman has to have. Many books have been devoted almost entirely to that subject, and I've seen some sales meetings where that was all the sales manager tried to produce.

Actually, when you become a pro, you almost automatically generate enthusiasm.

Complex, time-consuming sales-training methods based on theory rather than practice are resented by salesmen. I particularly dislike systems that show up a salesman's weaknesses in front of his employer and fellow salesmen. If they resist such instruction, who can blame them?

While we've tried to make the 20-Point System painless, there's one thing about it that hasn't been painless. You've had to think out your own solutions to your own selling problems. I'll bet you actually enjoyed that thinking before you got very far.

You're in a field where you need to be good. Consider what it costs your employer for you to make a sales call. If you don't already know the cost, try to find out. The amount will shock you.

Consider the number of days a week you work—usually five. Consider the time spent in setting up appointments, the time spent on planning calls, the cost of the selling aids you're given, the time spent between calls in getting from place to place, the cost of transportation and other travel expenses, your salary, administrative costs, reports, time spent waiting for unexpectedly busy prospects—the amount gets to be staggering, and the hours you spend in actual selling come down to comparatively few a day.

Of those few hours when you're trying to close business, you can't afford to waste a minute. At least, your employer can't afford to have you waste it.

The salesman who does a superior job, day in and day out, is so rare that he's regarded as one of the company's greatest assets. He usually goes to the top like a skyrocket, in both money and status.

You be that fellow—a sales pro!

Index